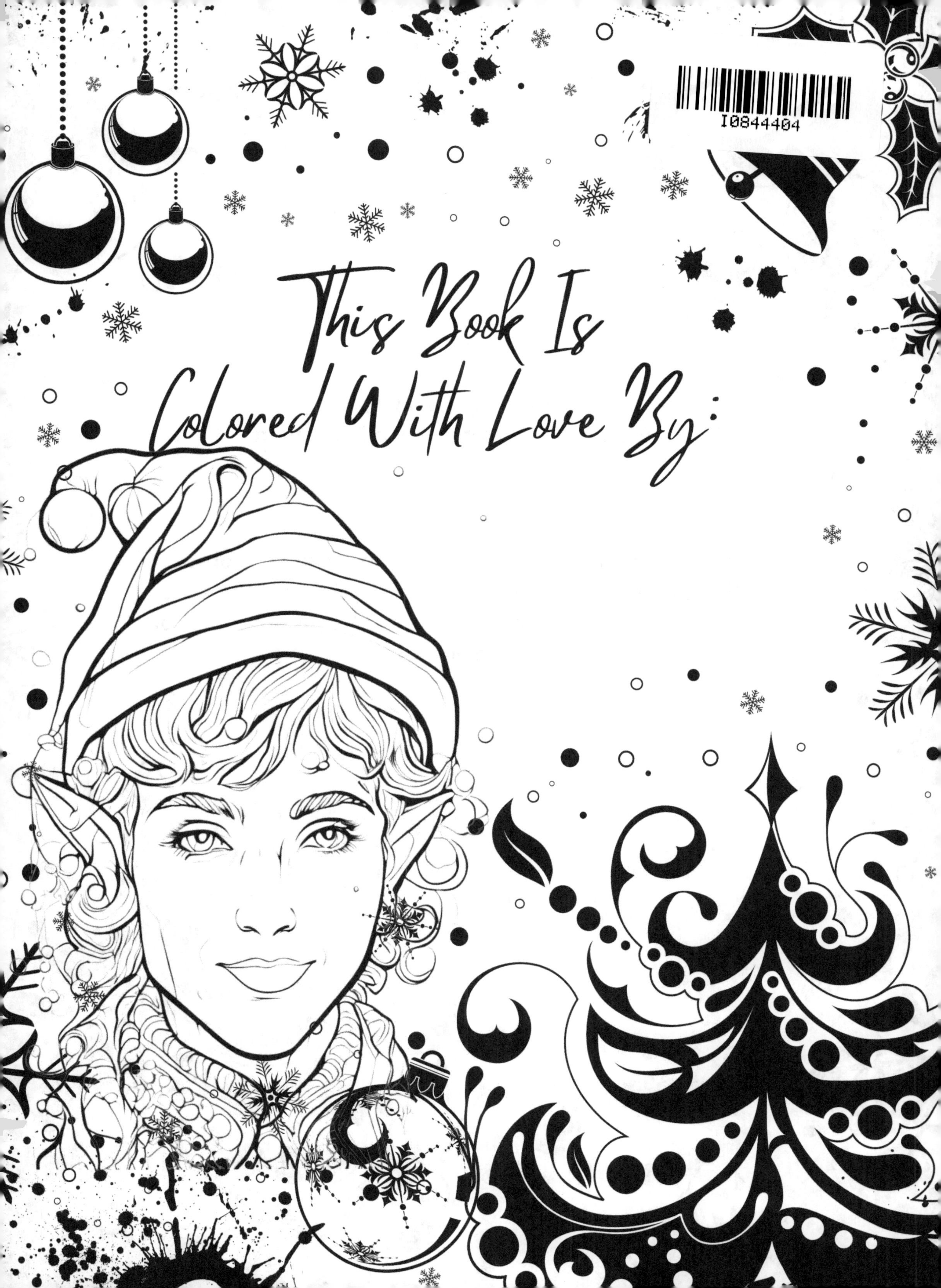
This Book Is
Colored With Love By:
I0844404

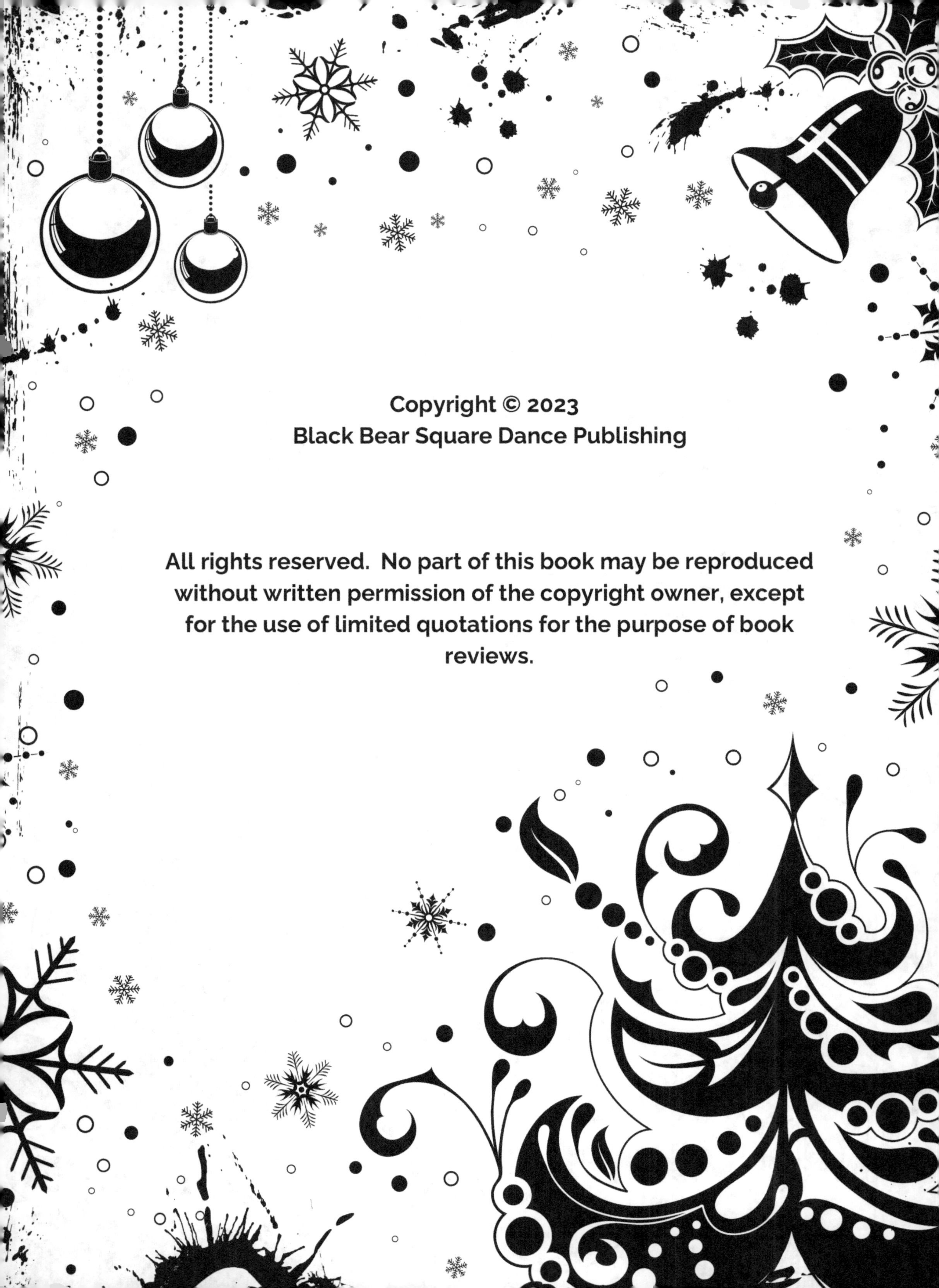

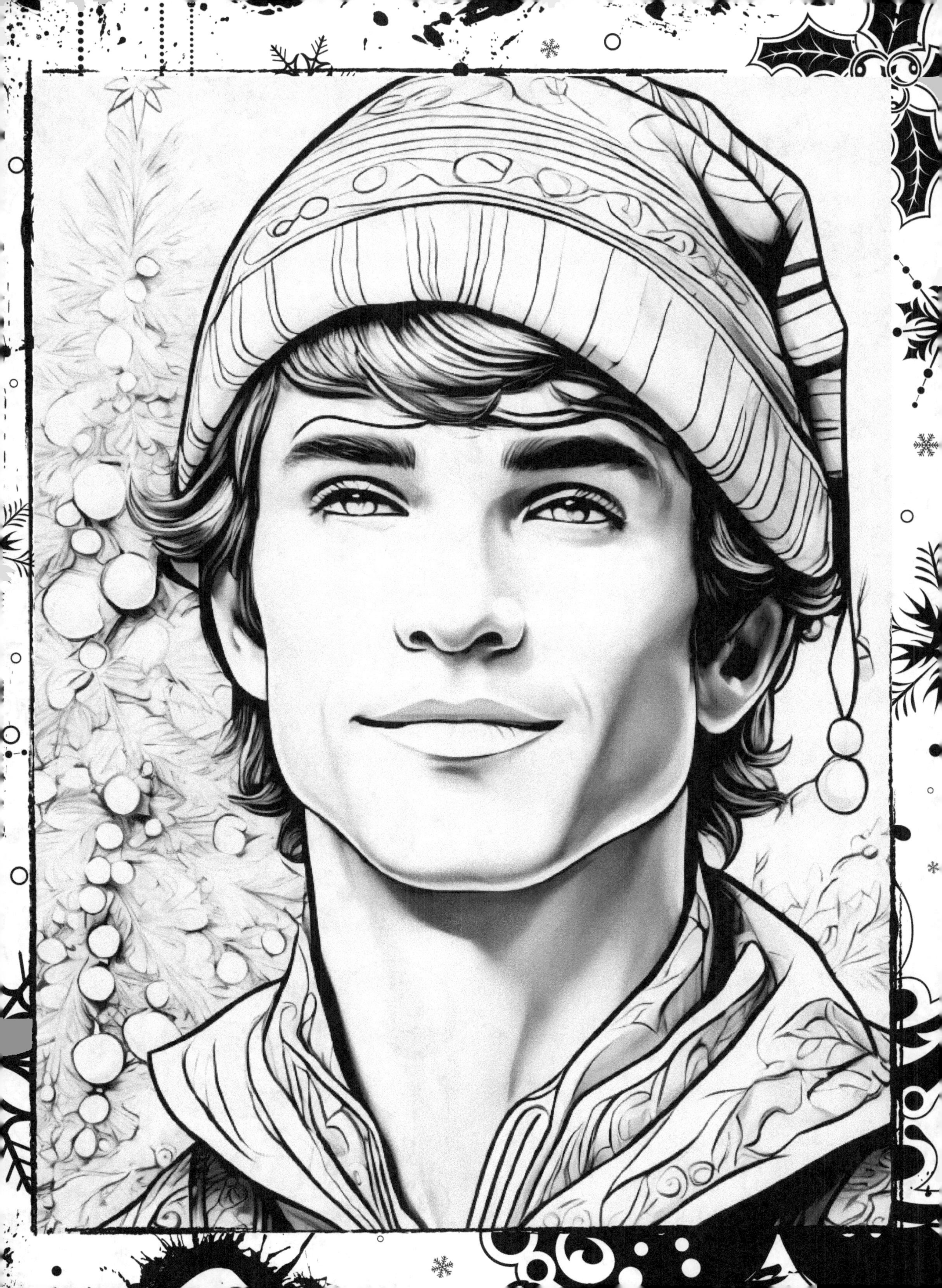

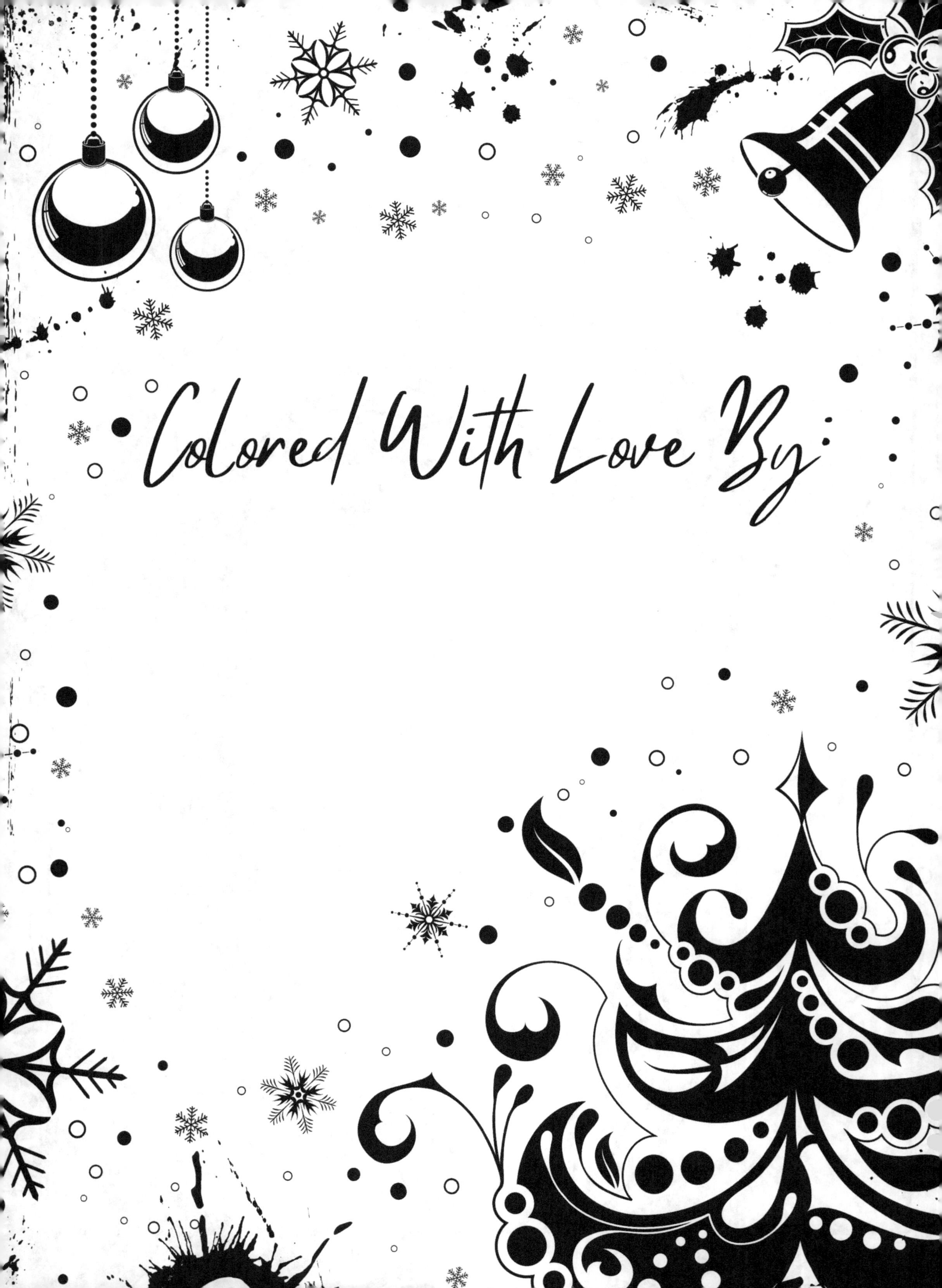

Colored With Love By:

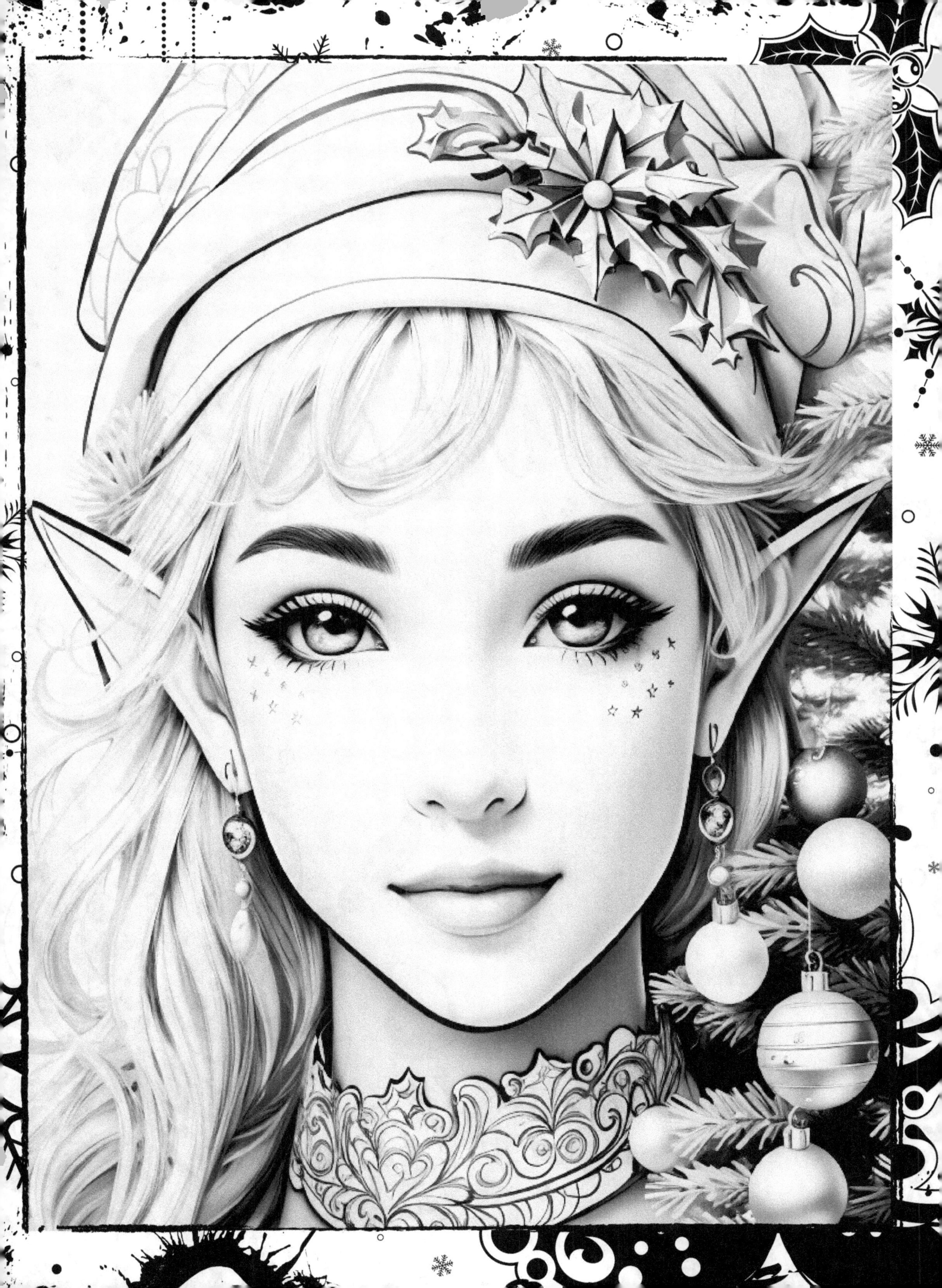

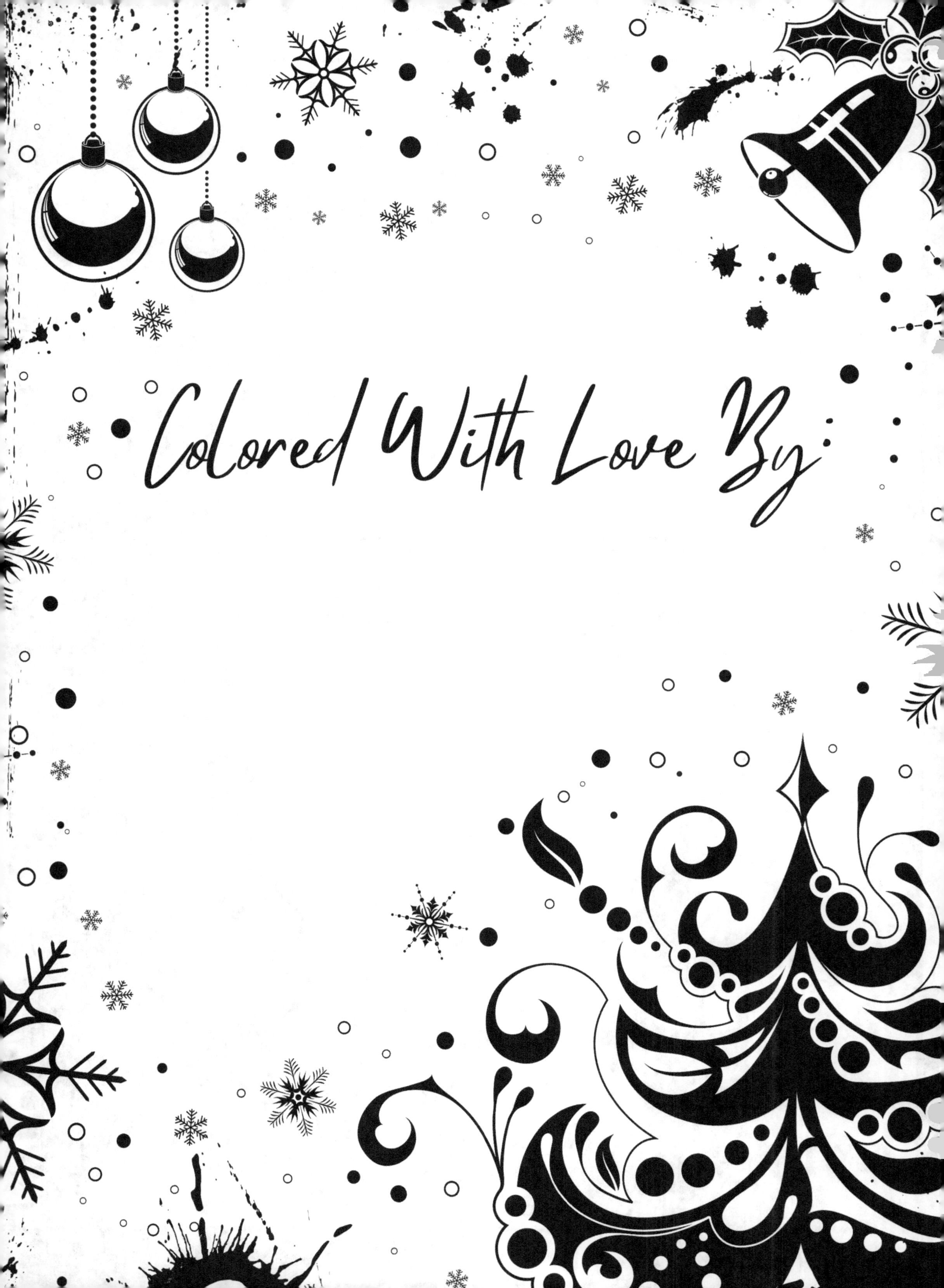

Colored With Love By:

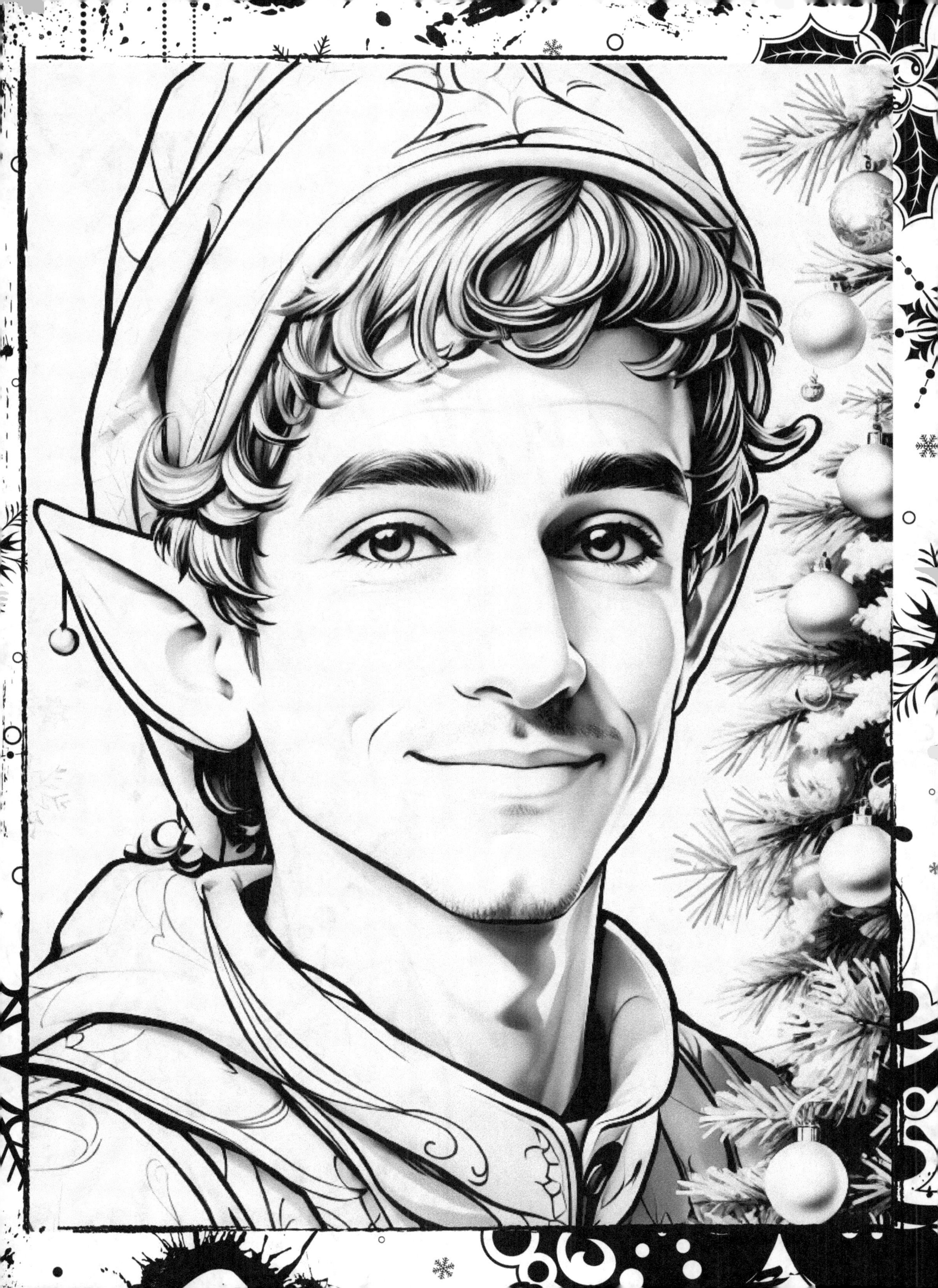

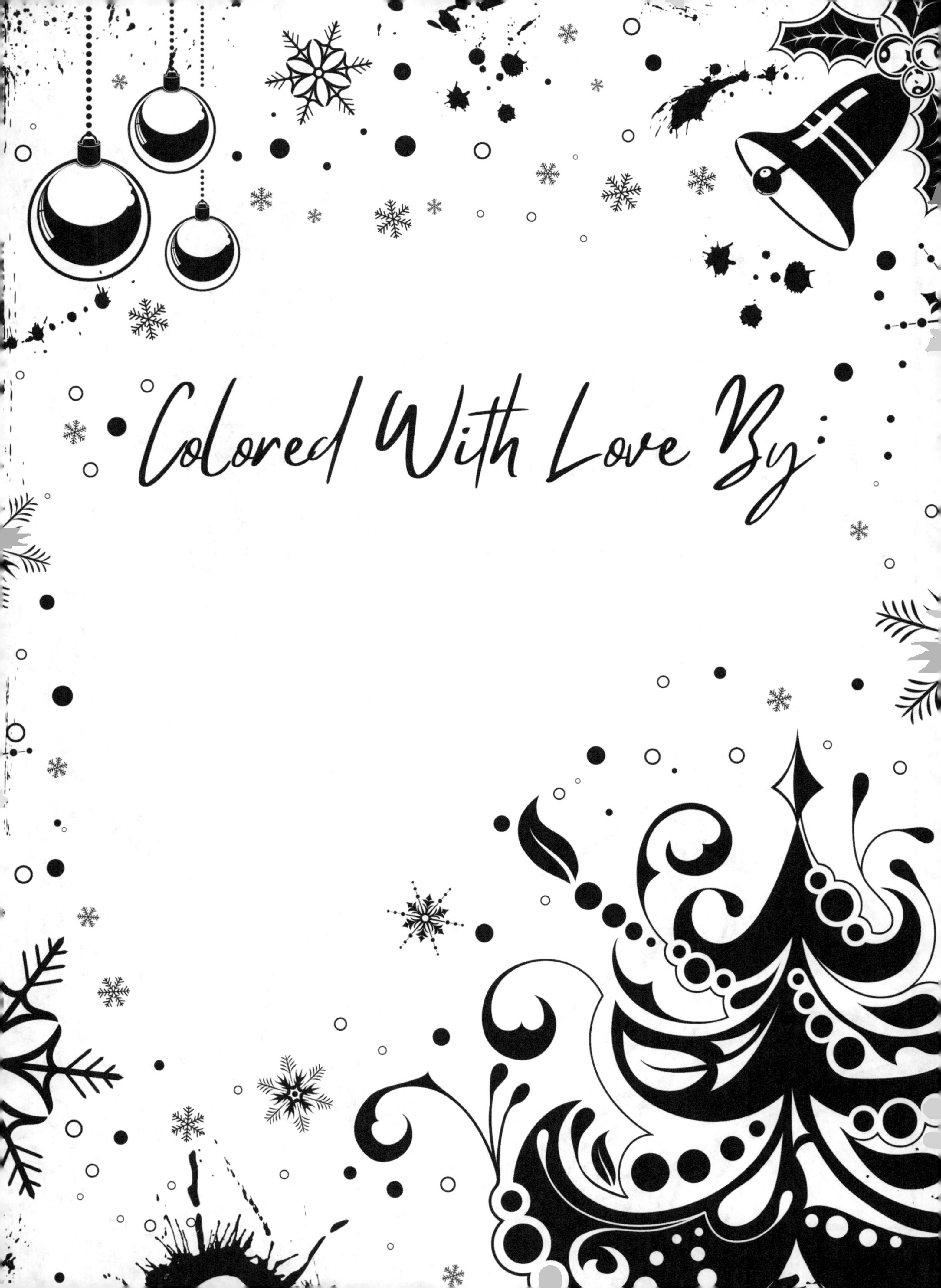

Colored With Love By:

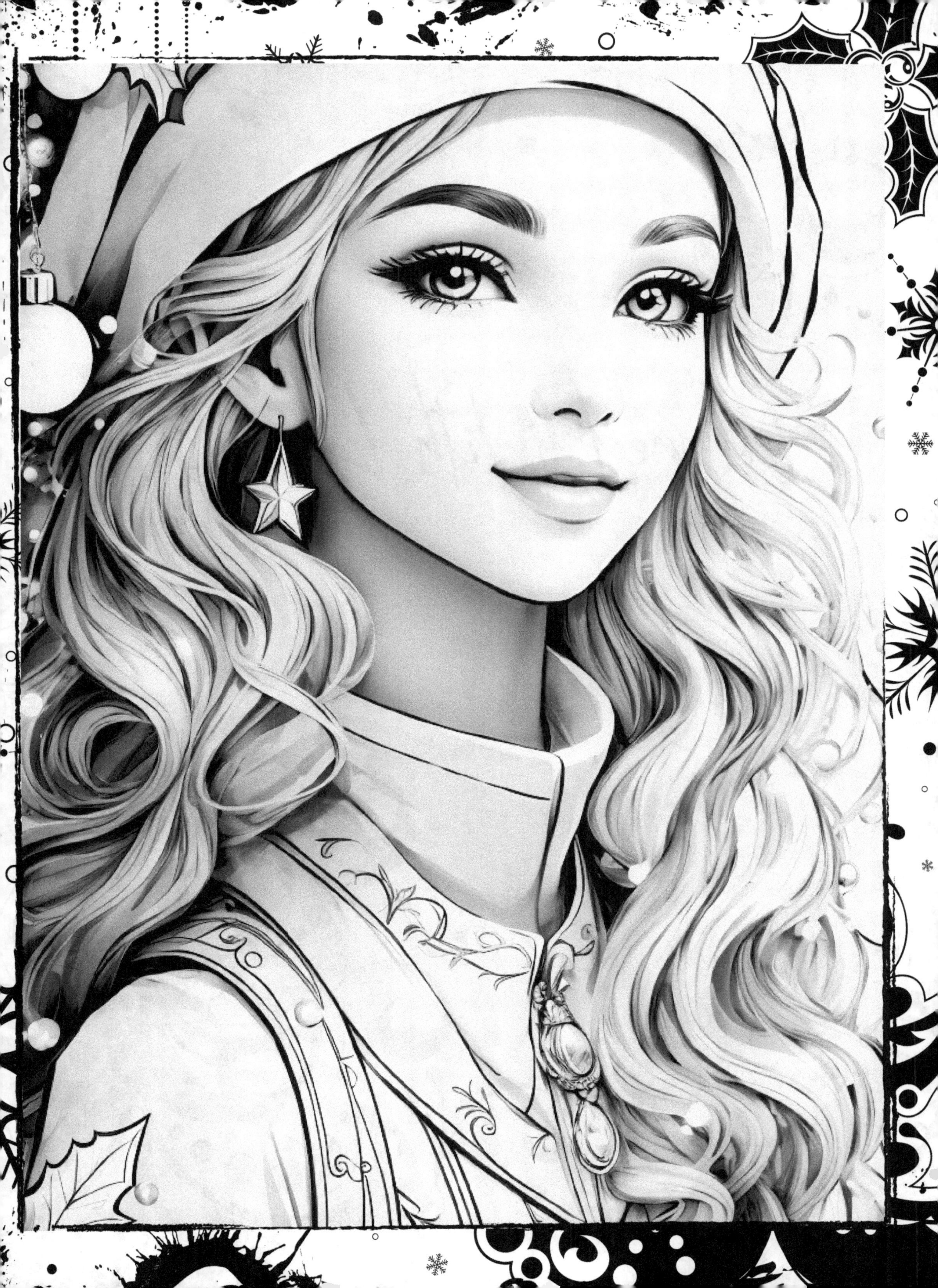

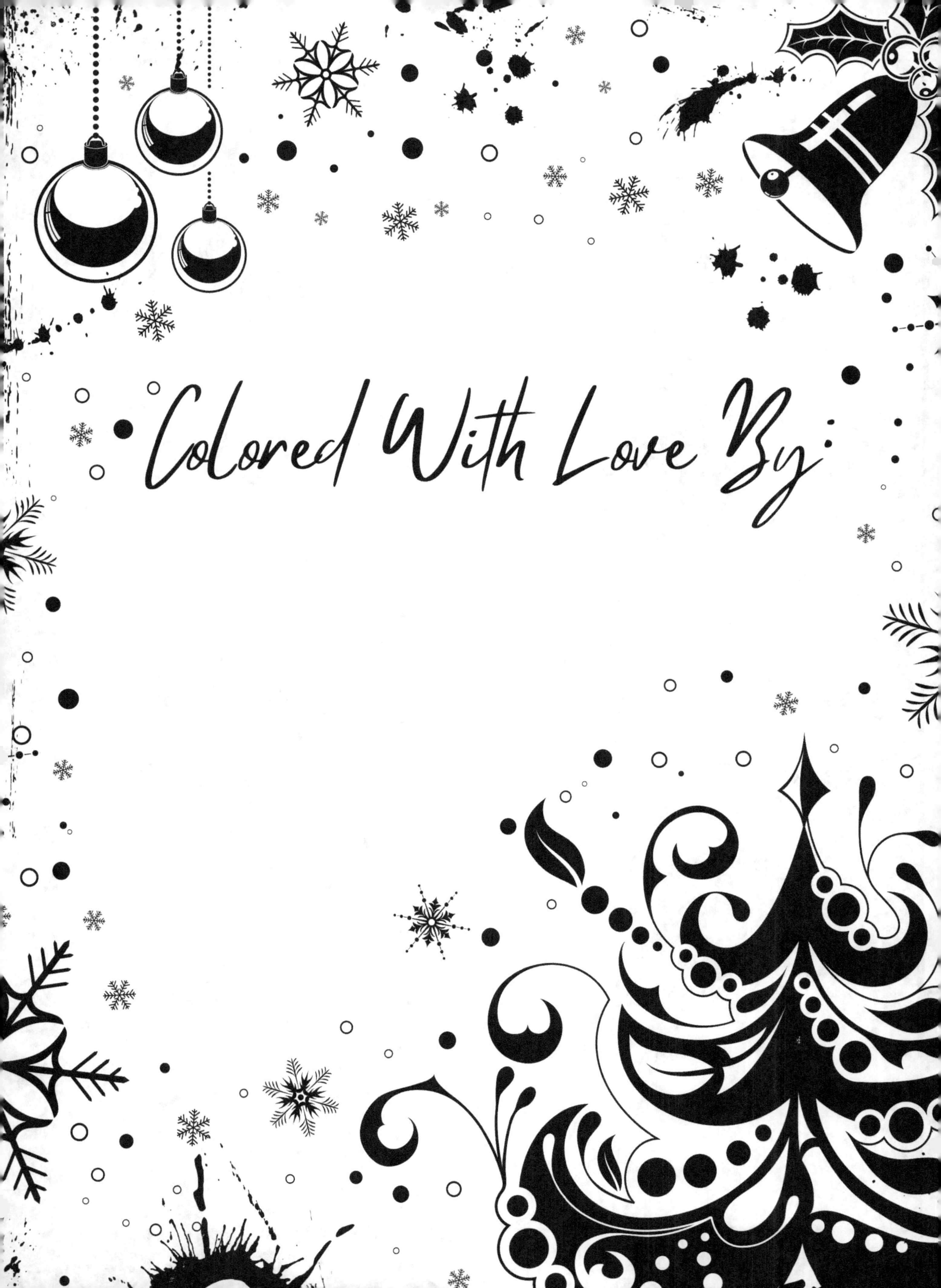

Colored With Love By:

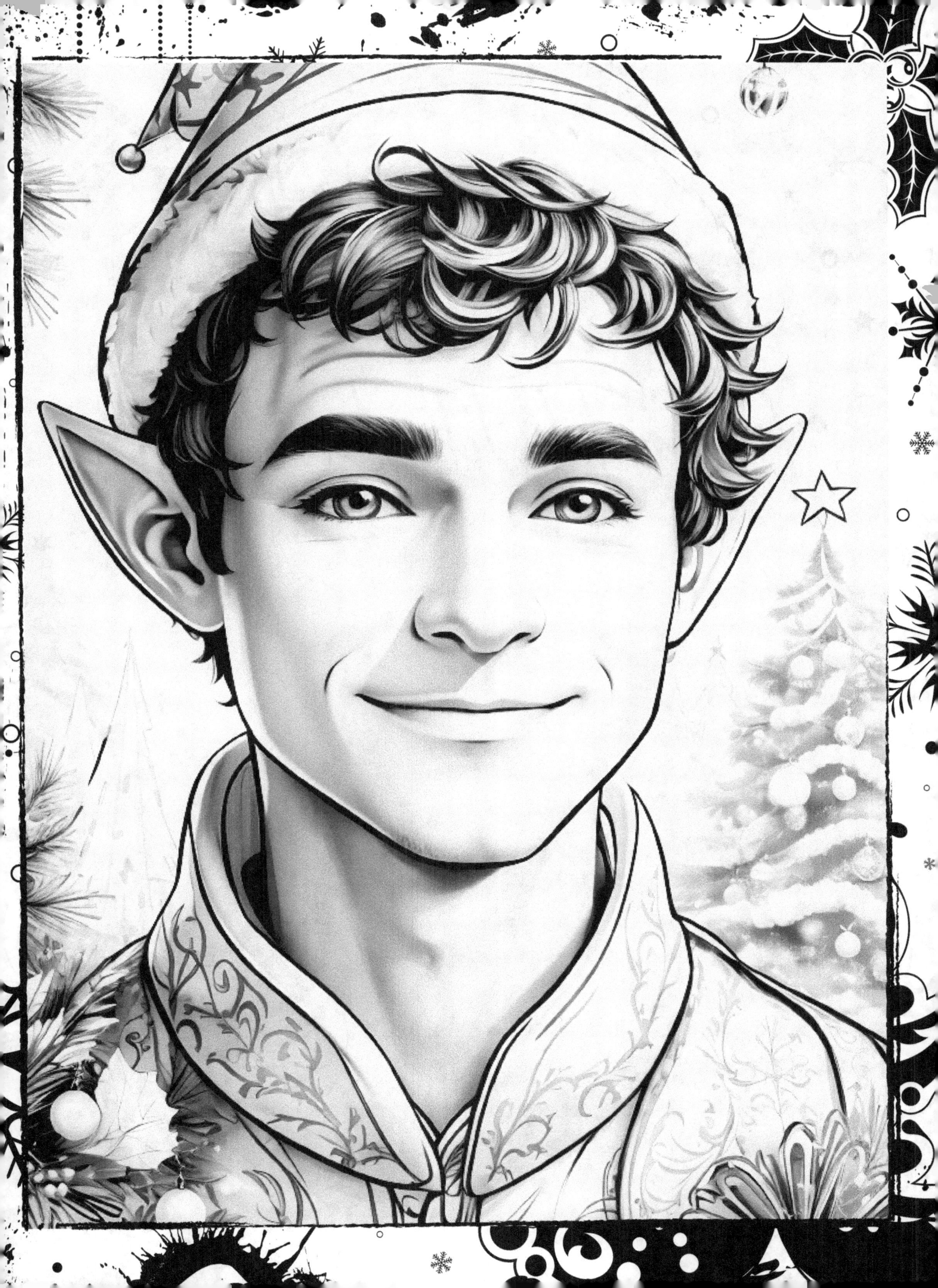

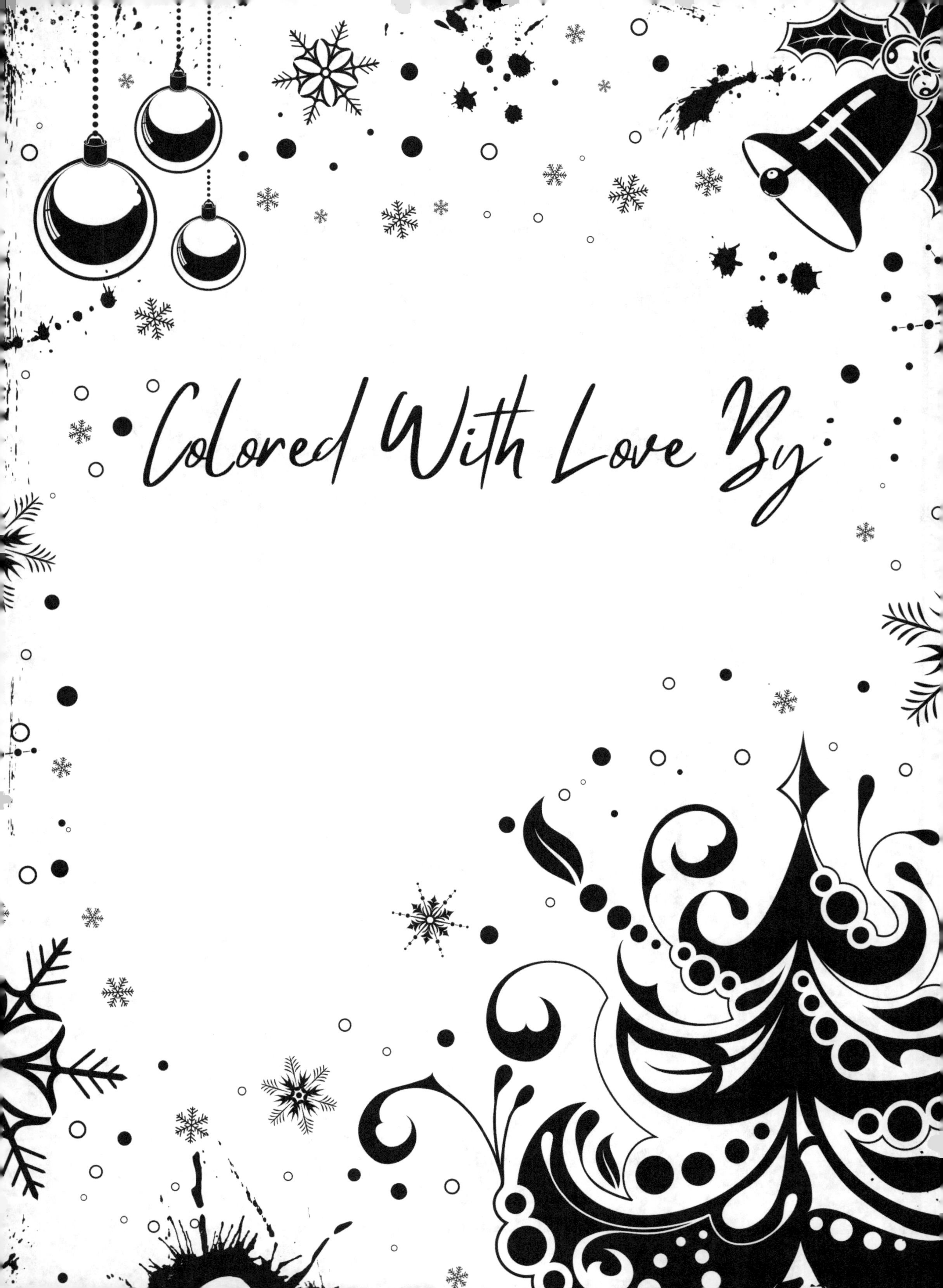

Colored With Love By:

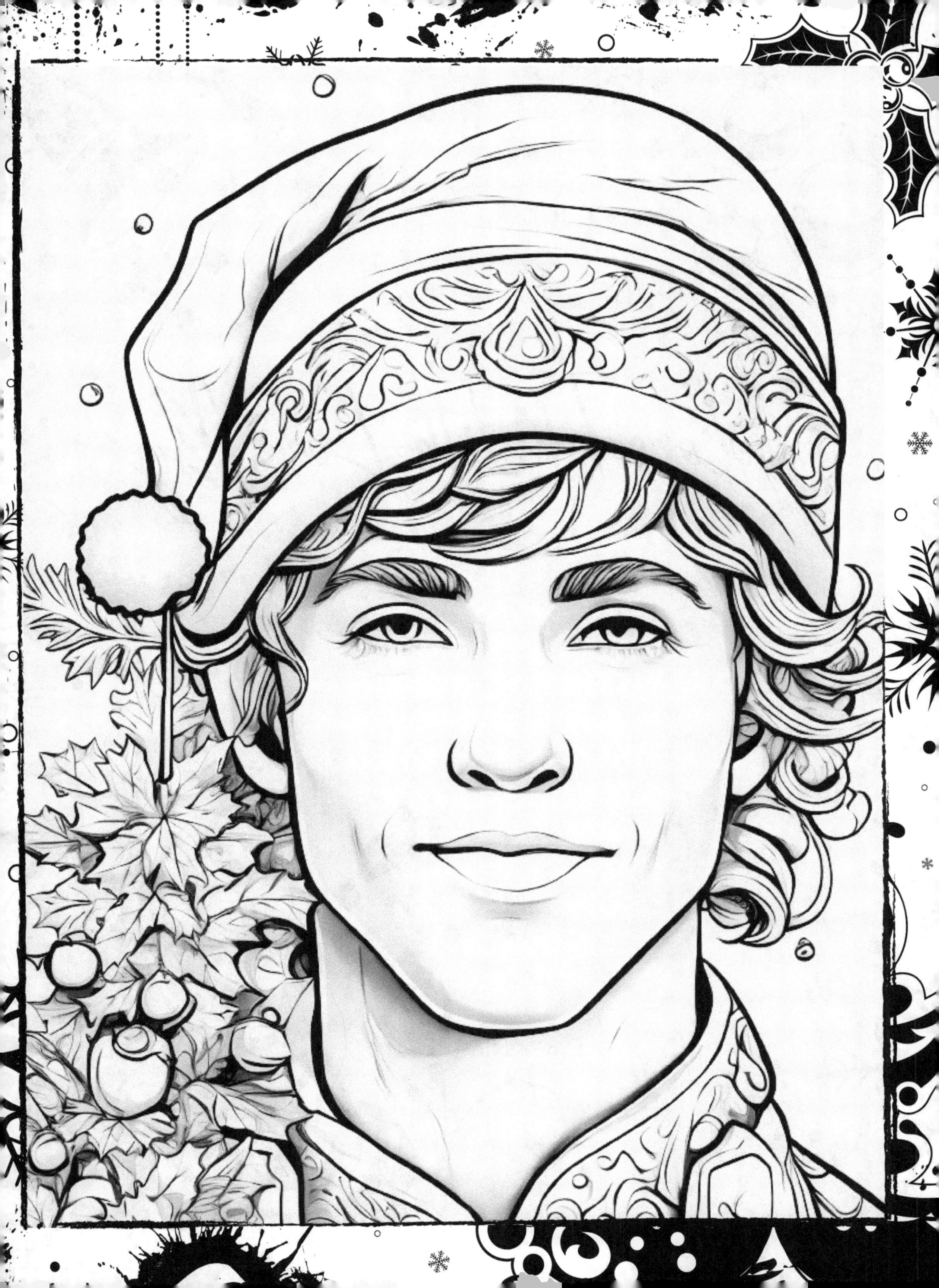

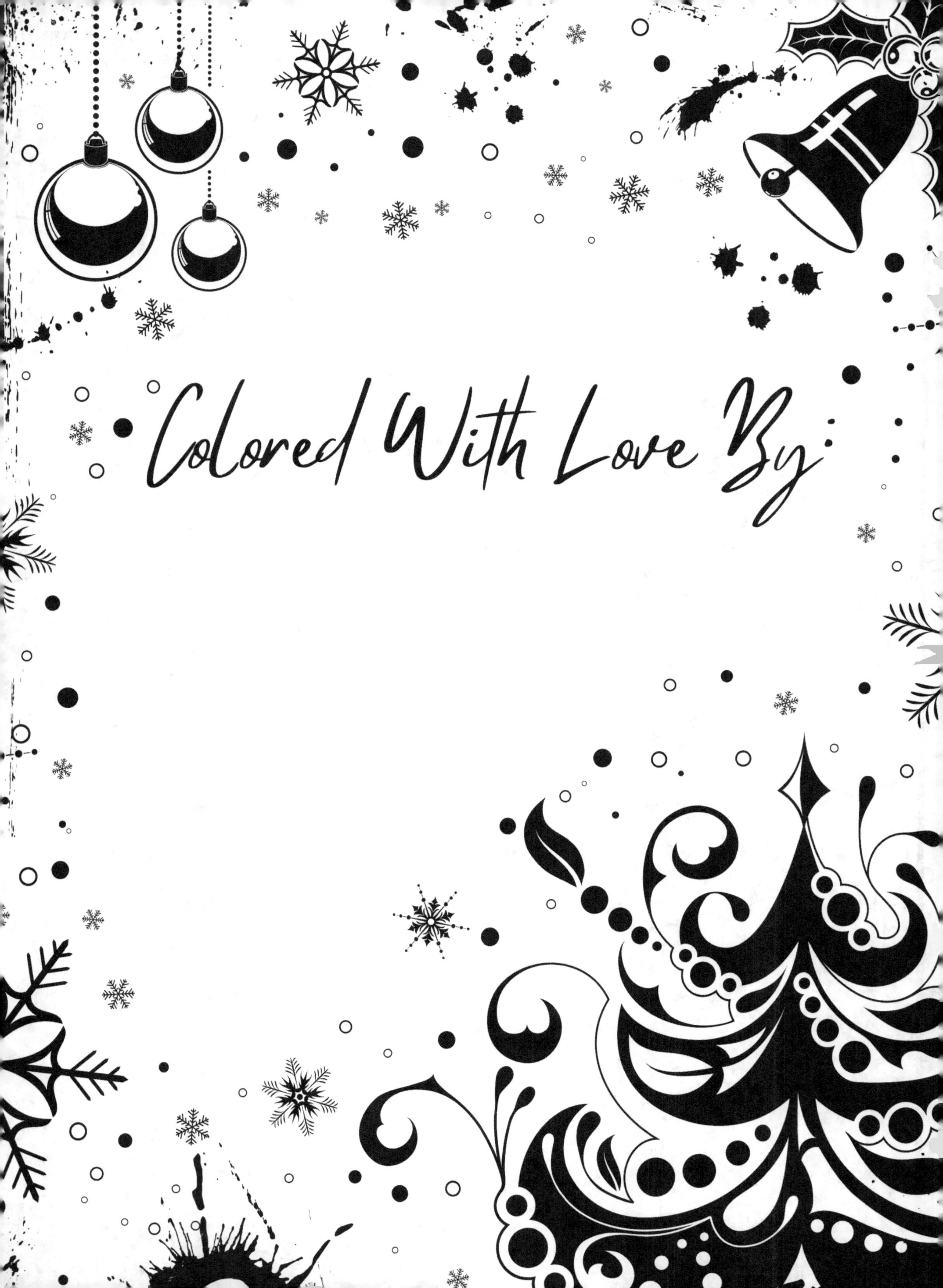

Colored With Love By:

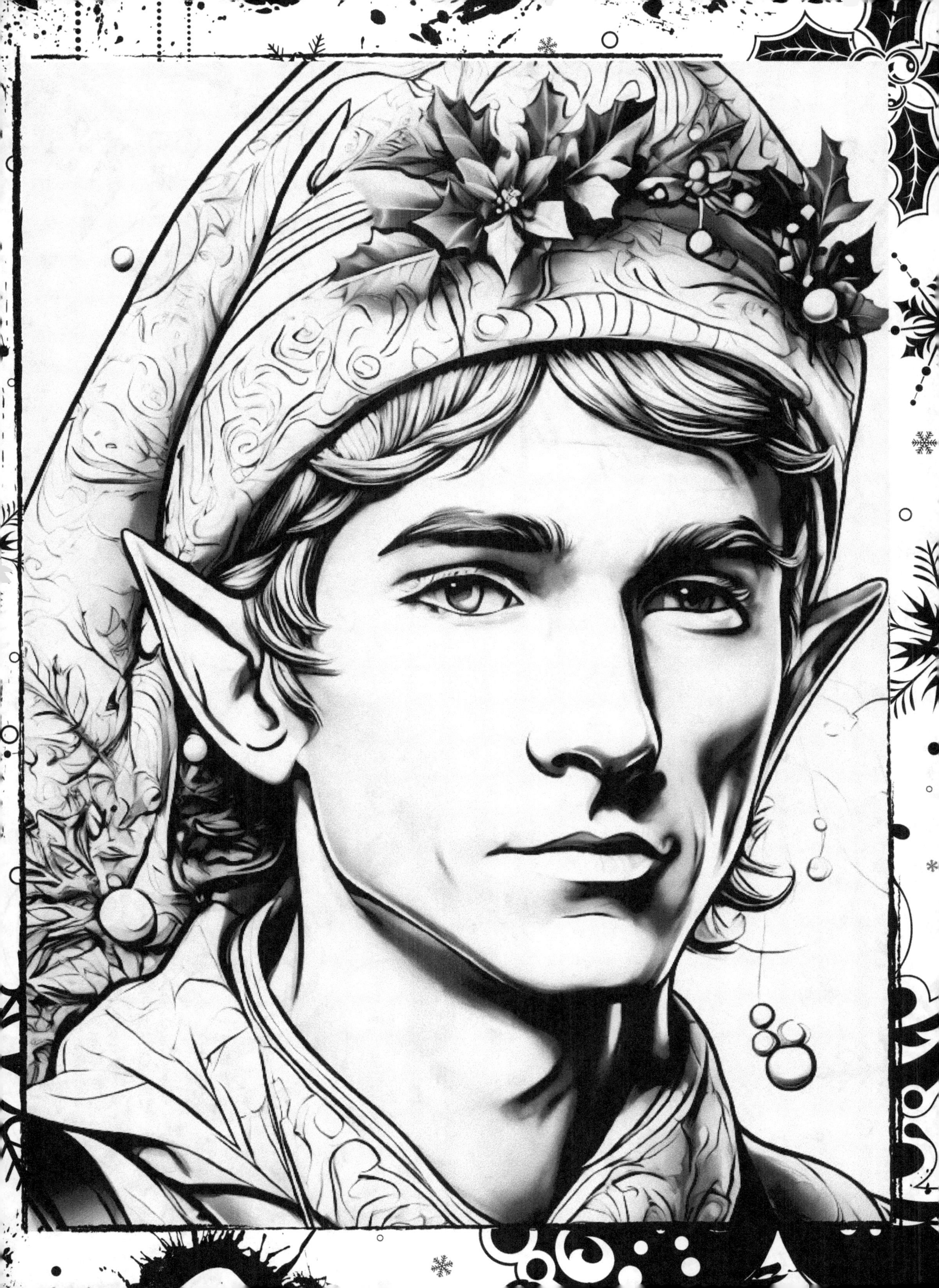

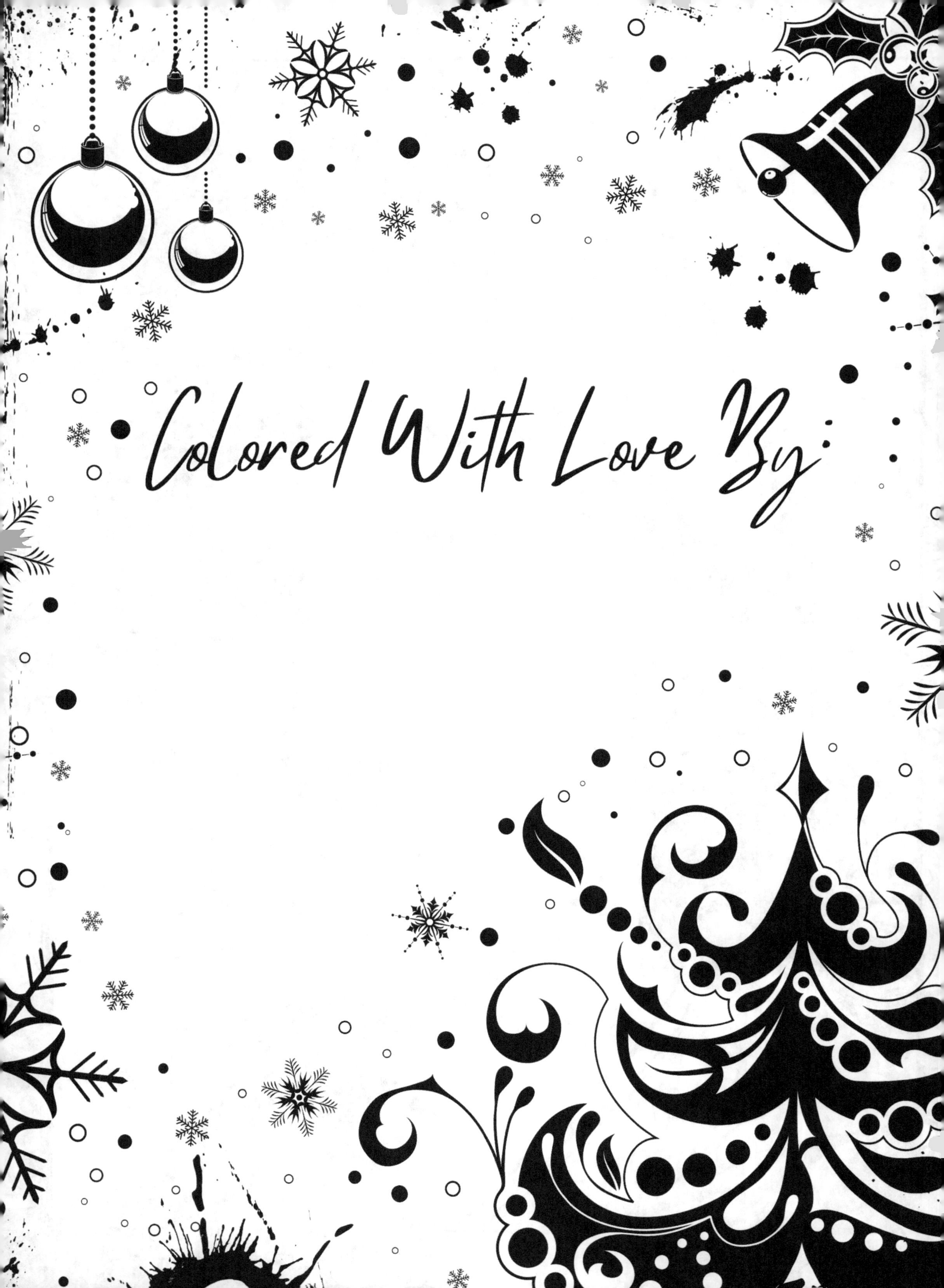
Colored With Love By:

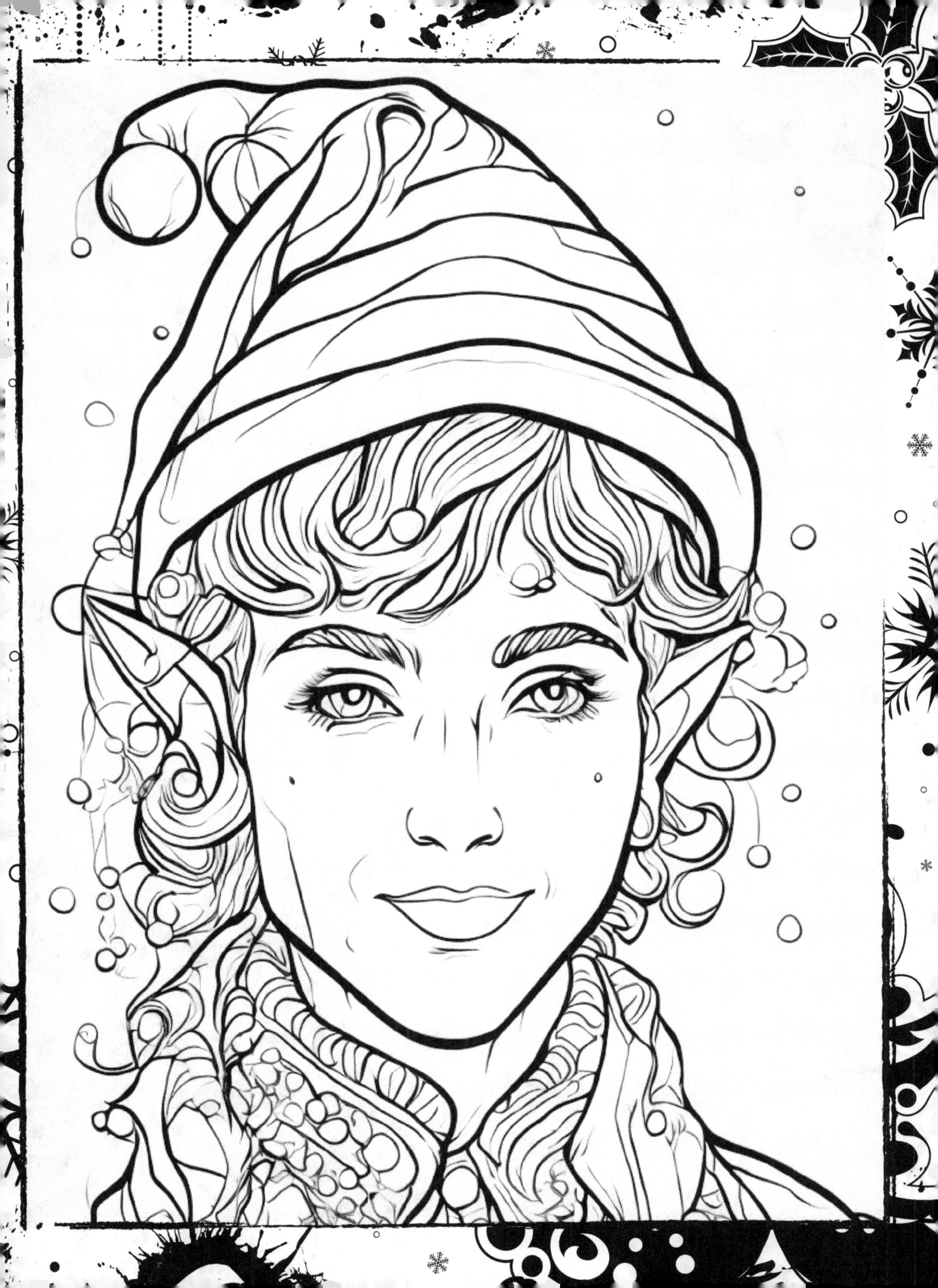

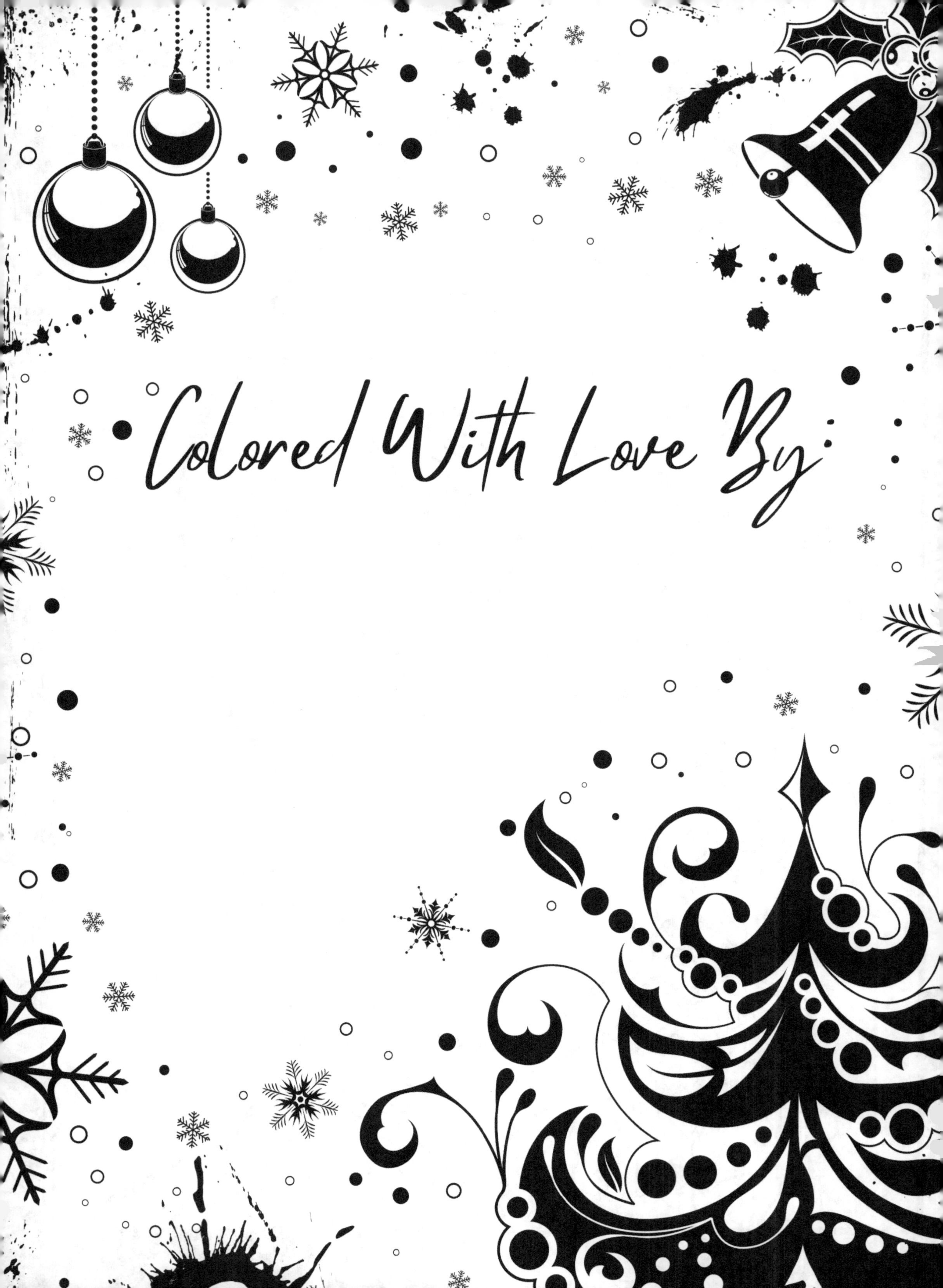
Colored With Love By:

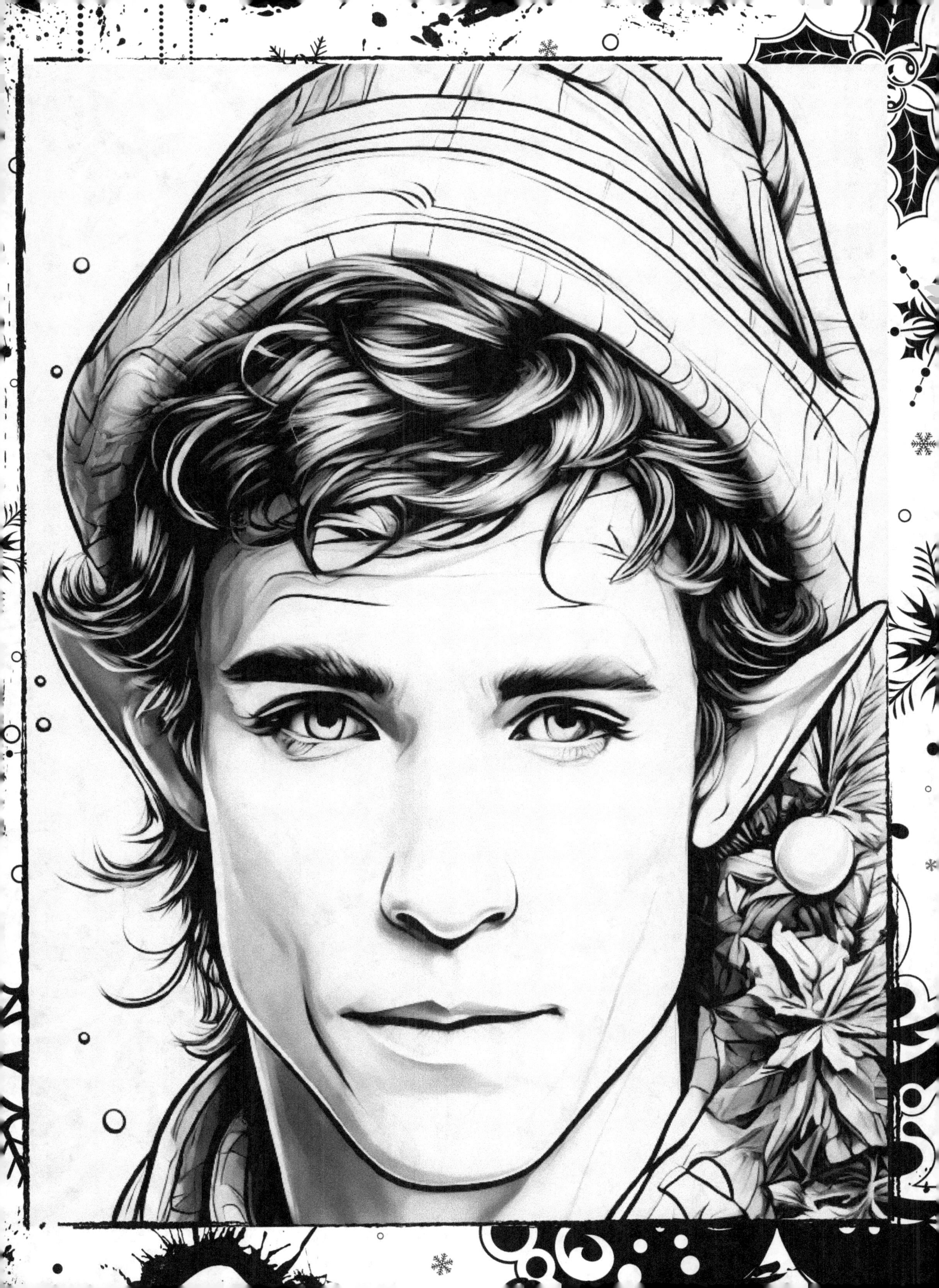

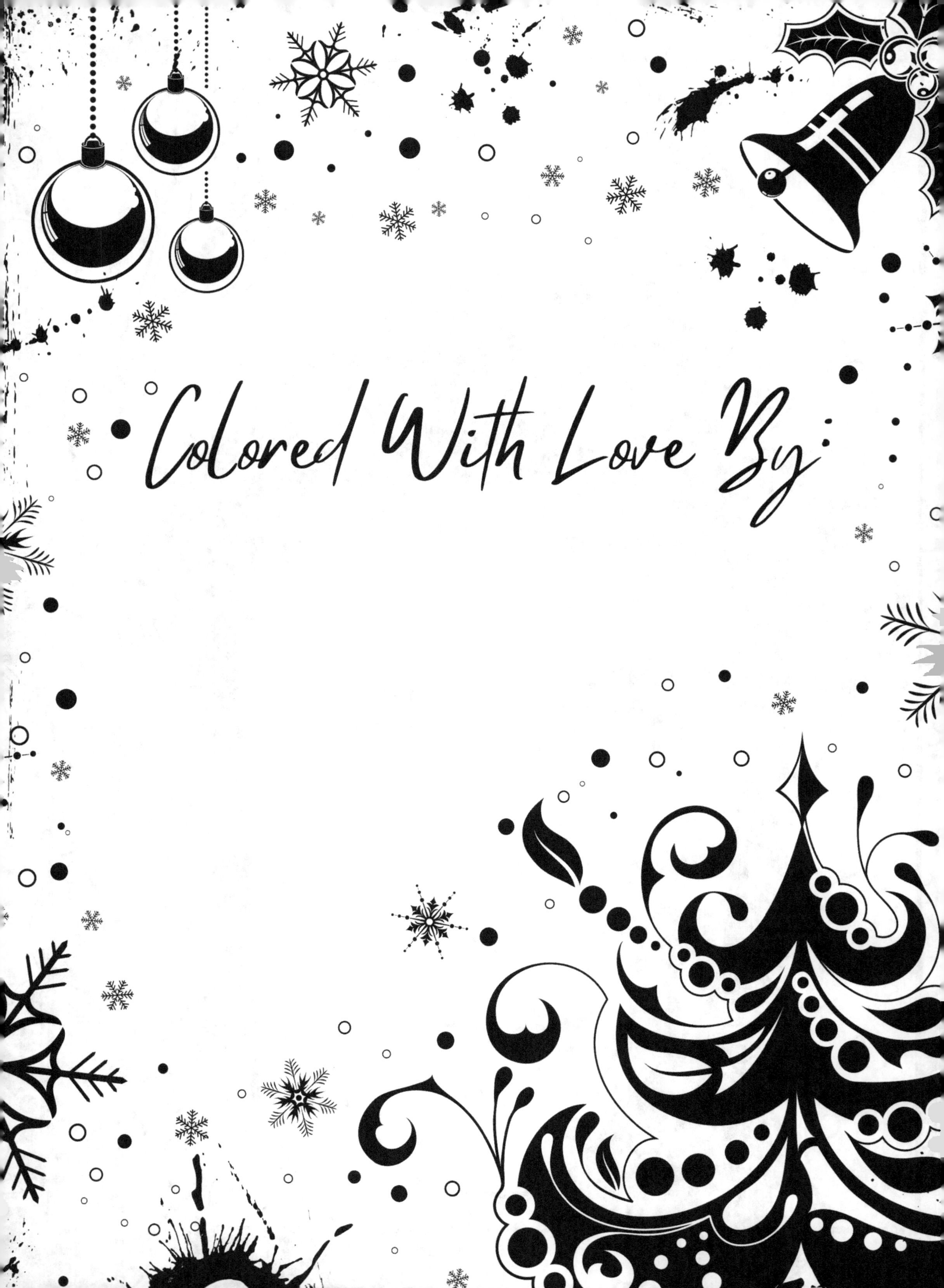
Colored With Love By:

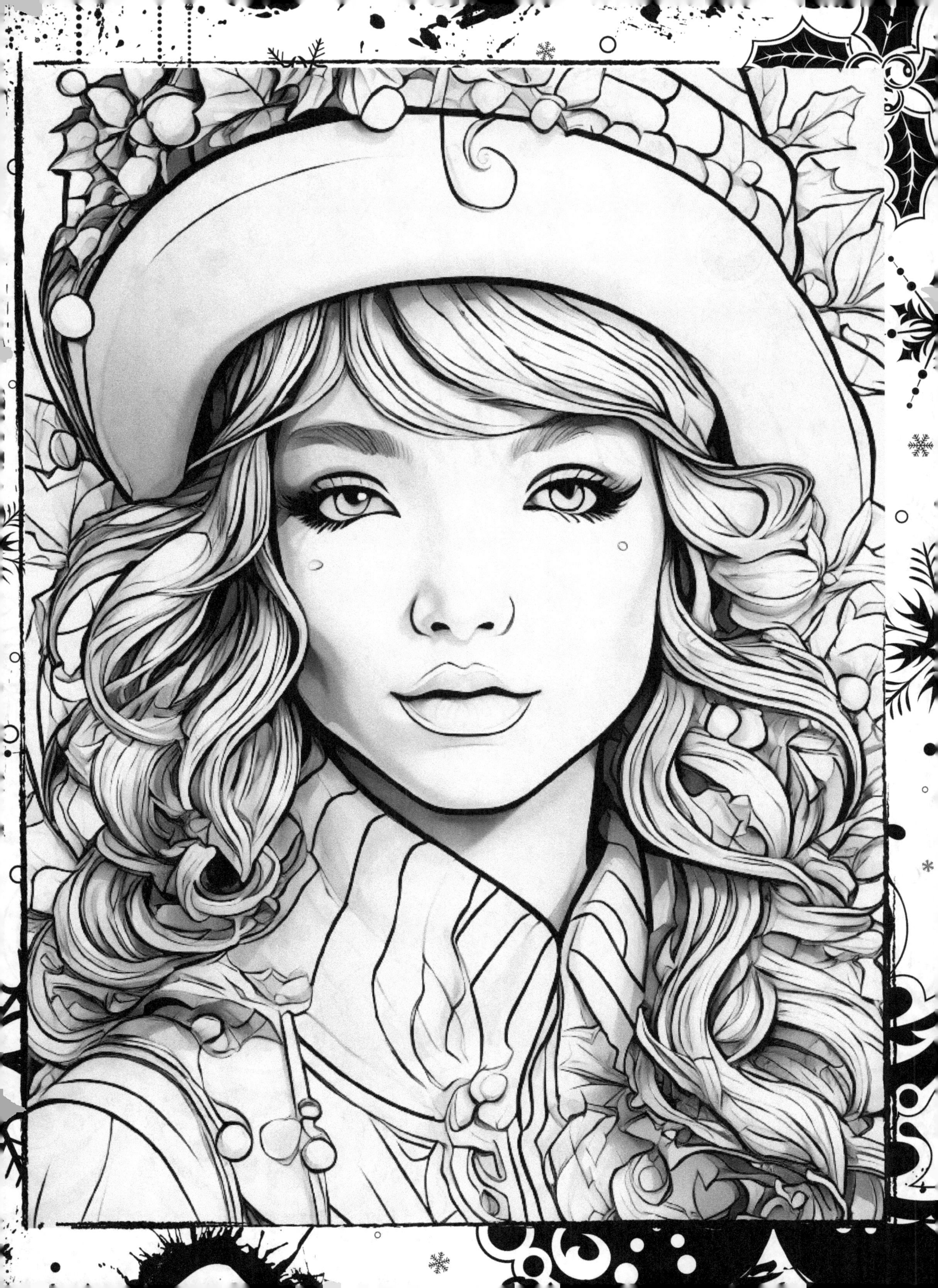

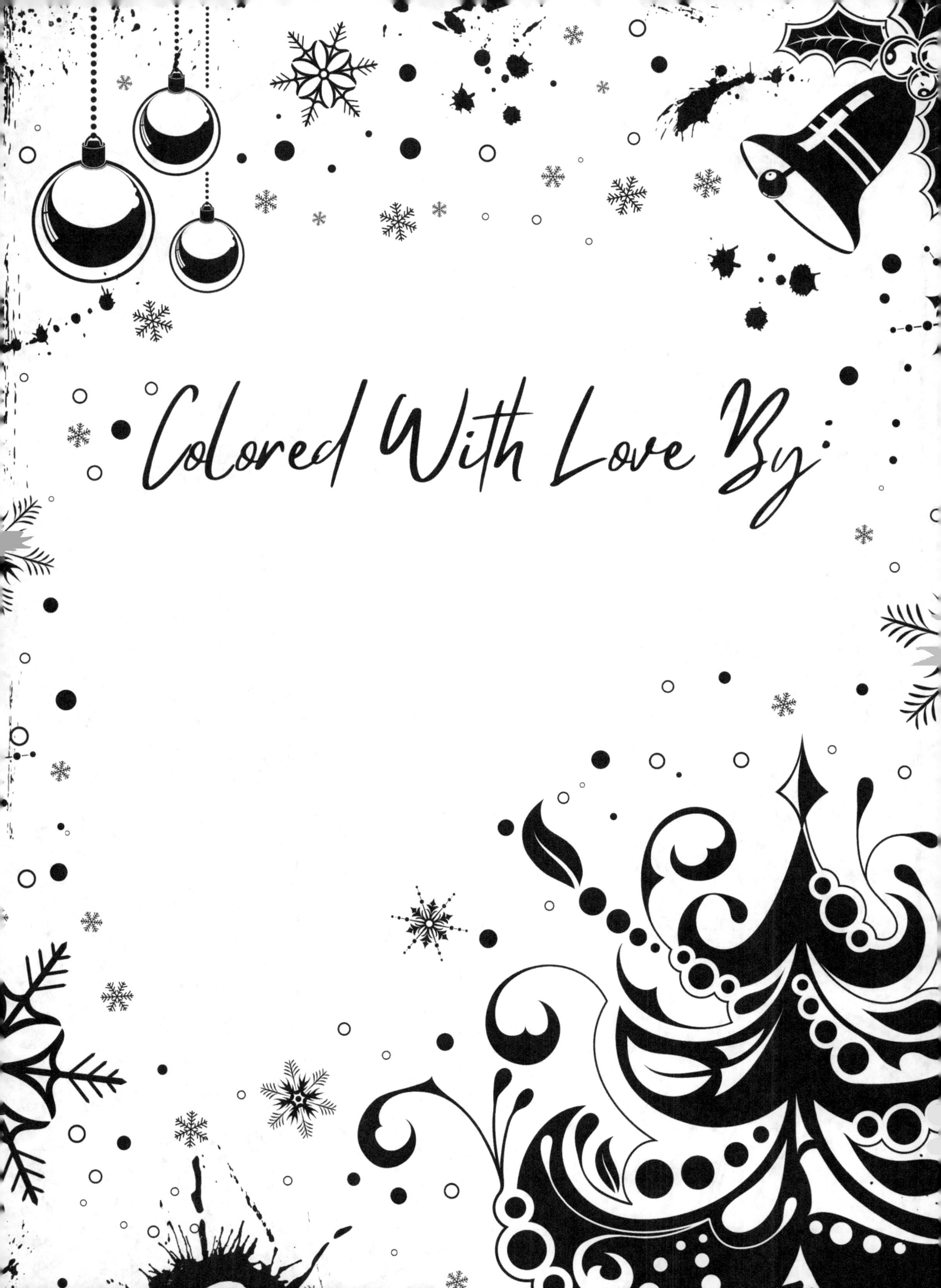
Colored With Love By:

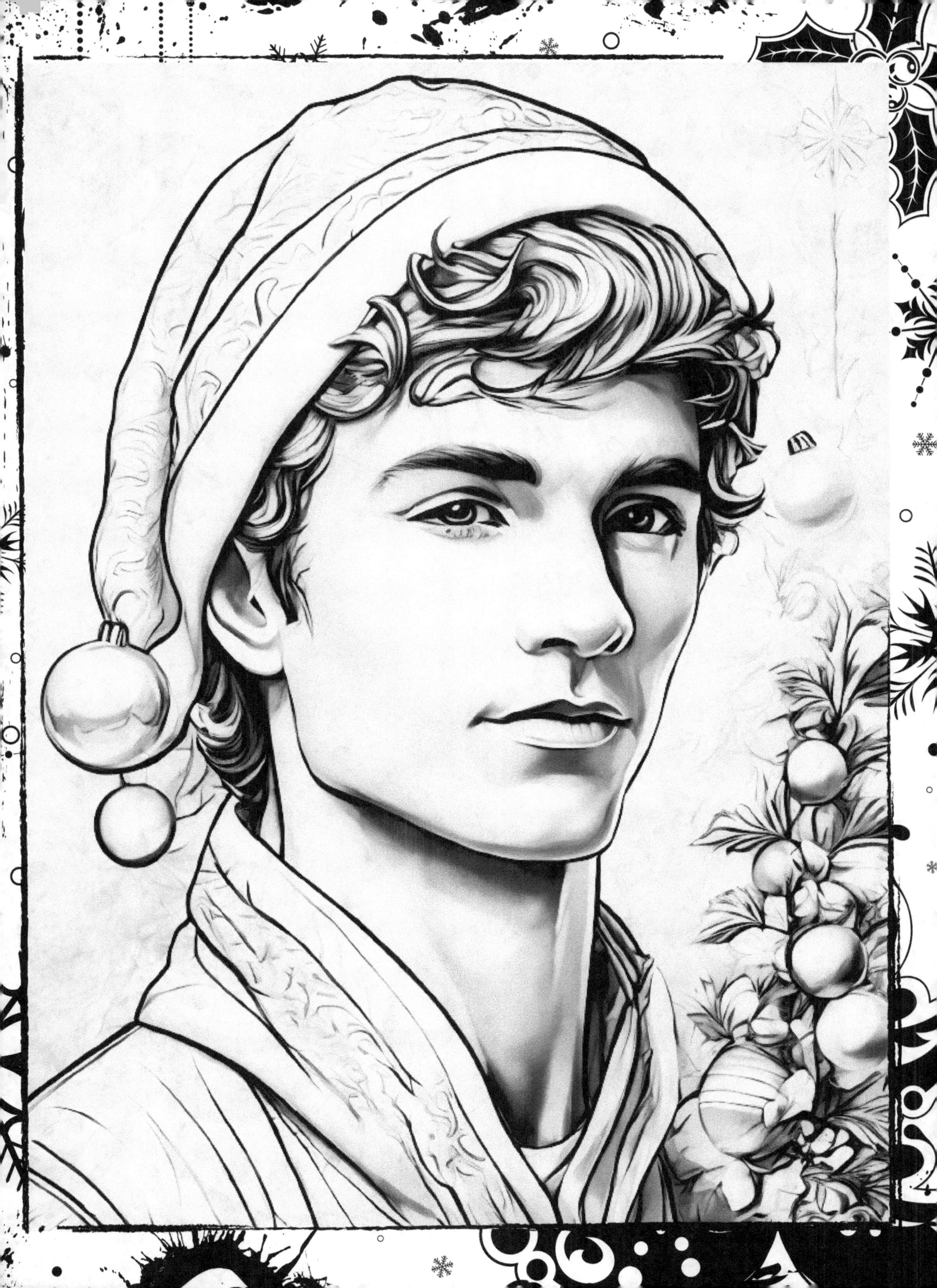

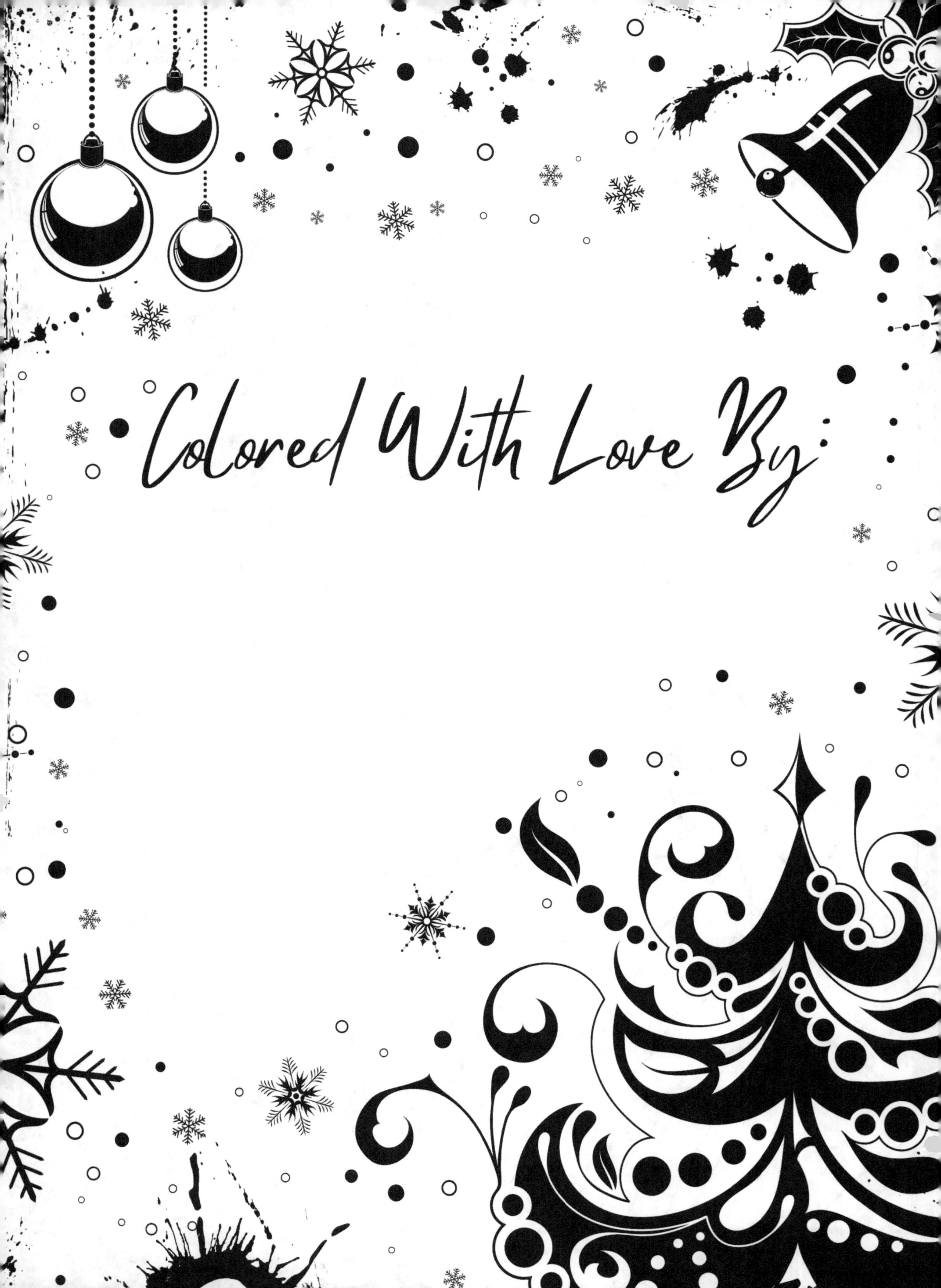
Colored With Love By:

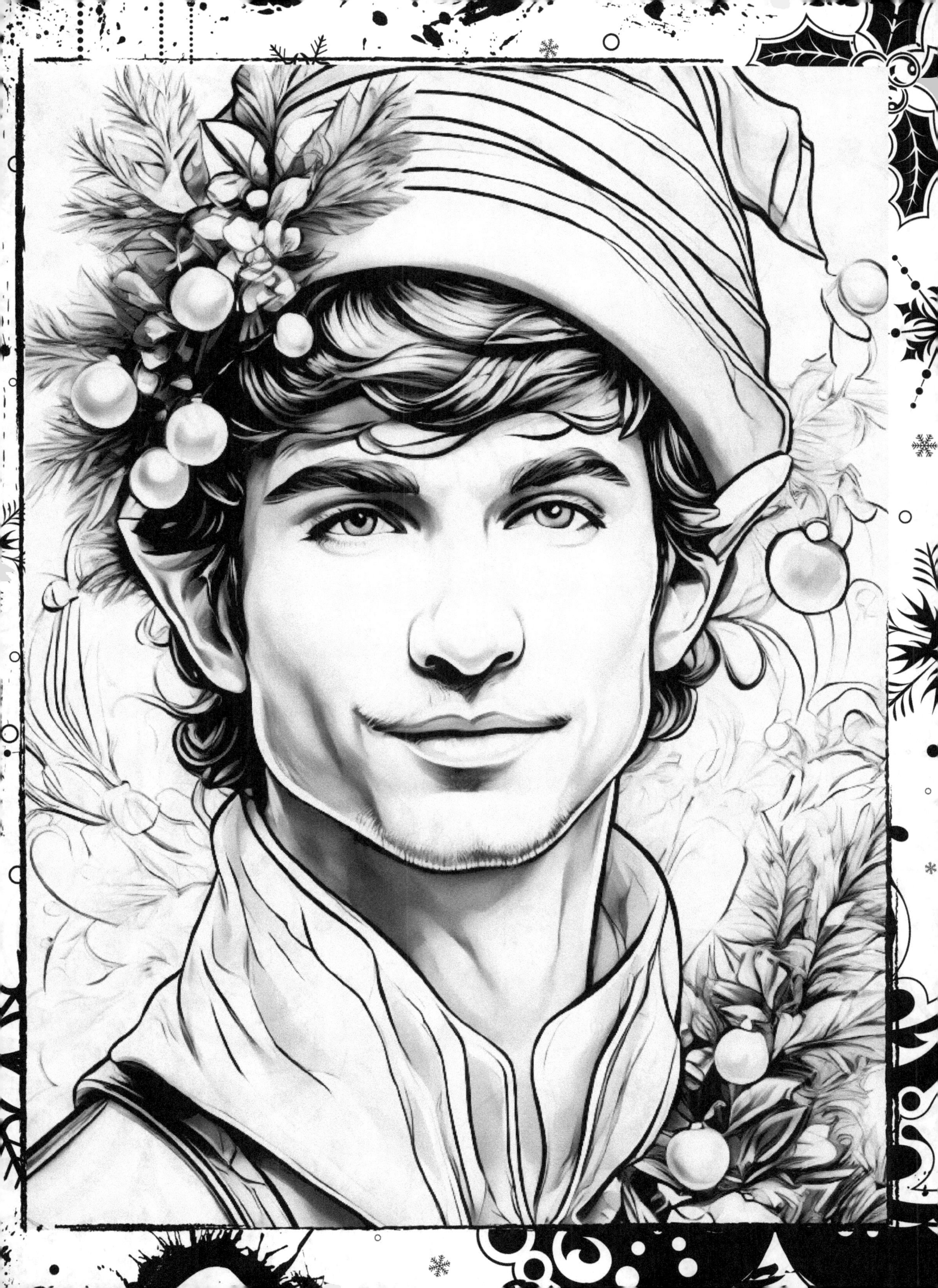

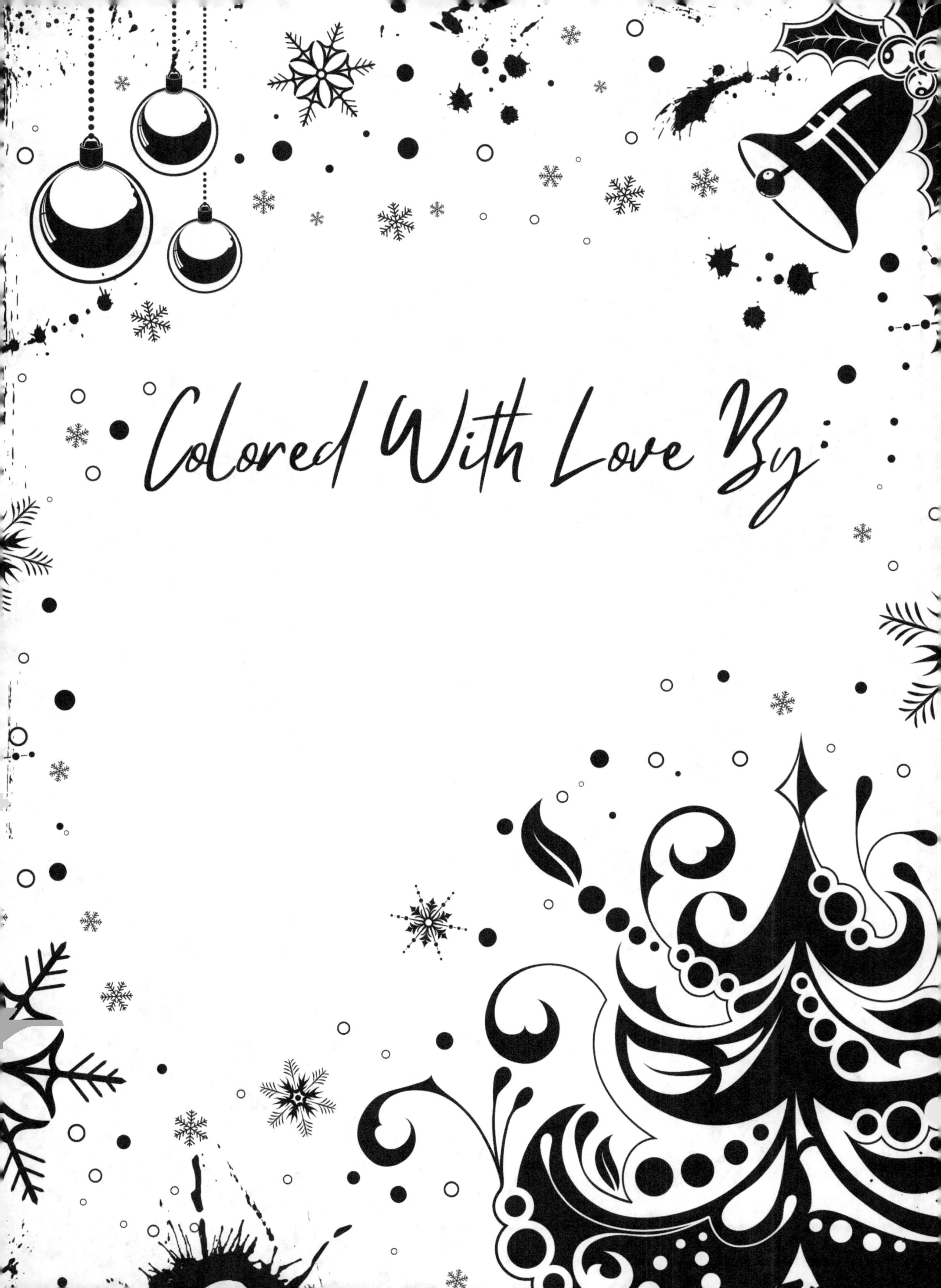
Colored With Love By:

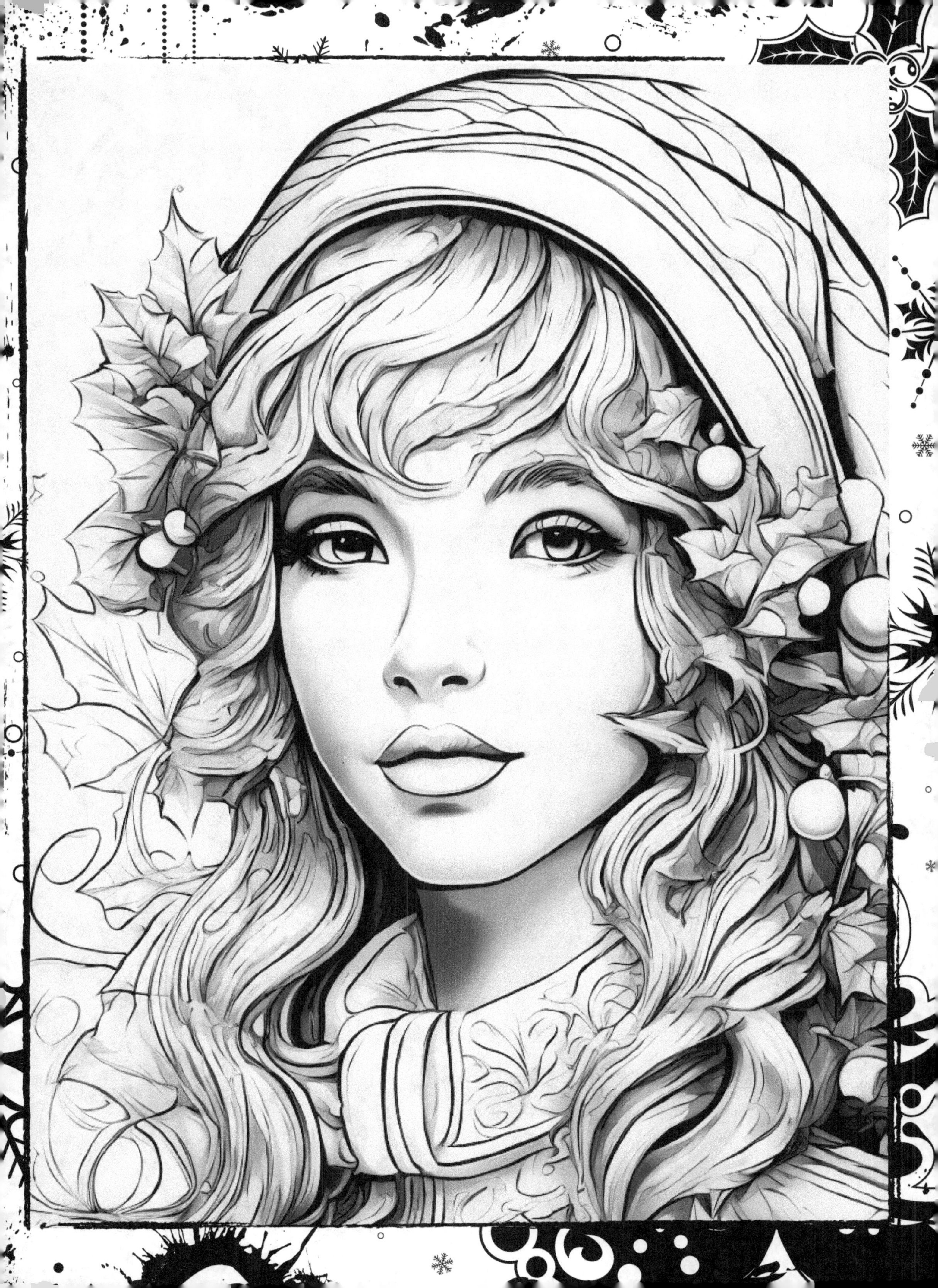

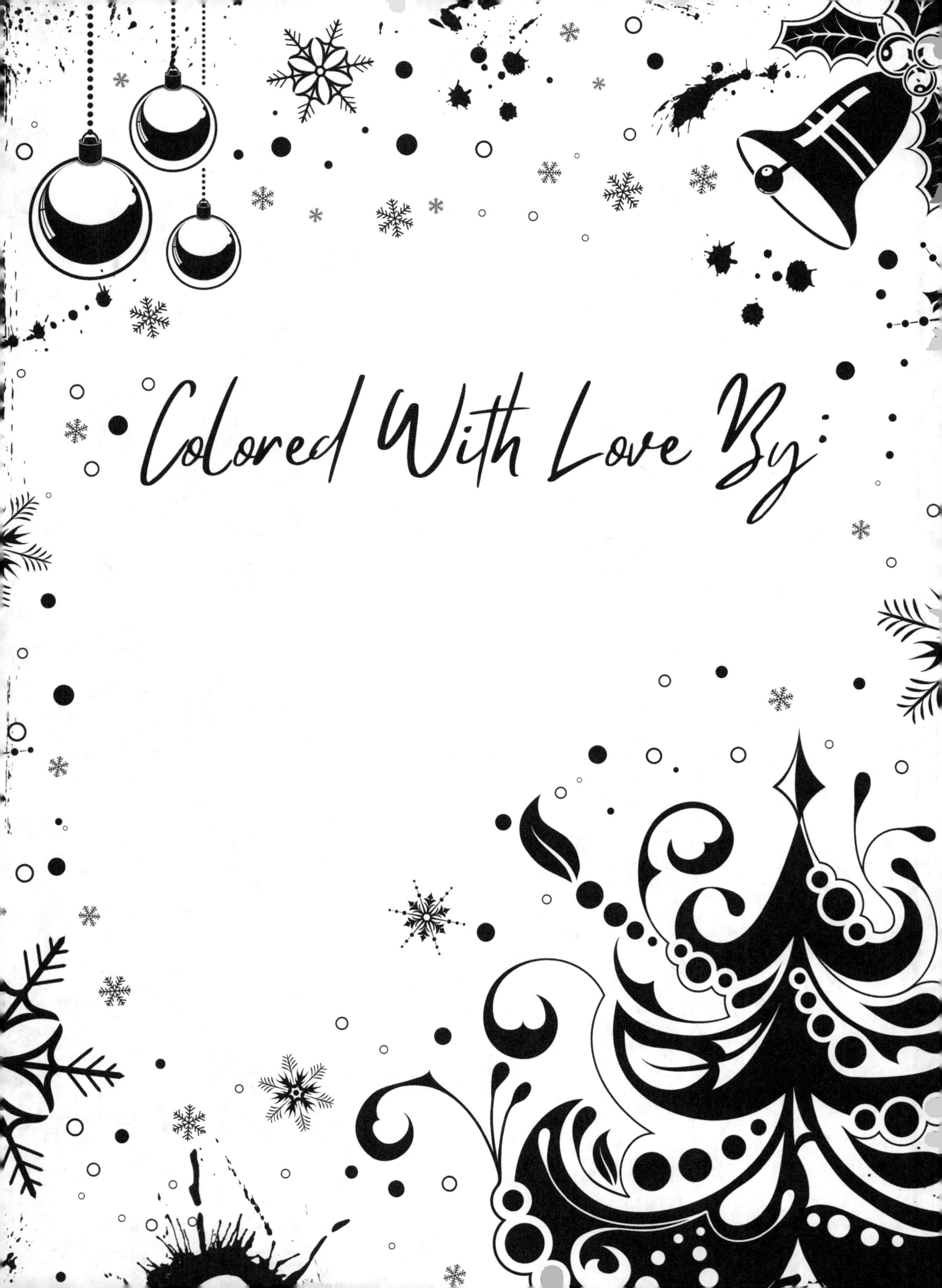
Colored With Love By:

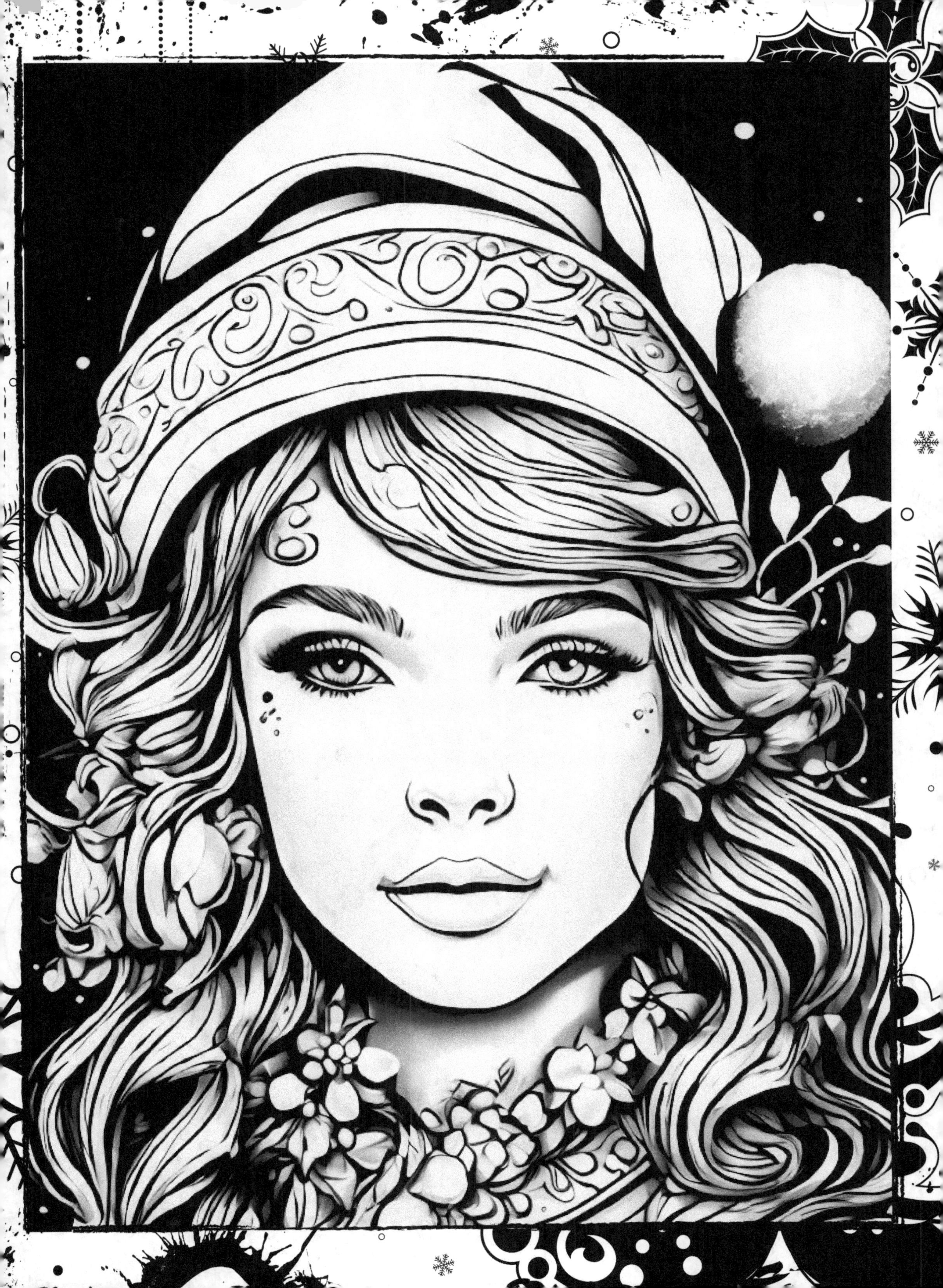

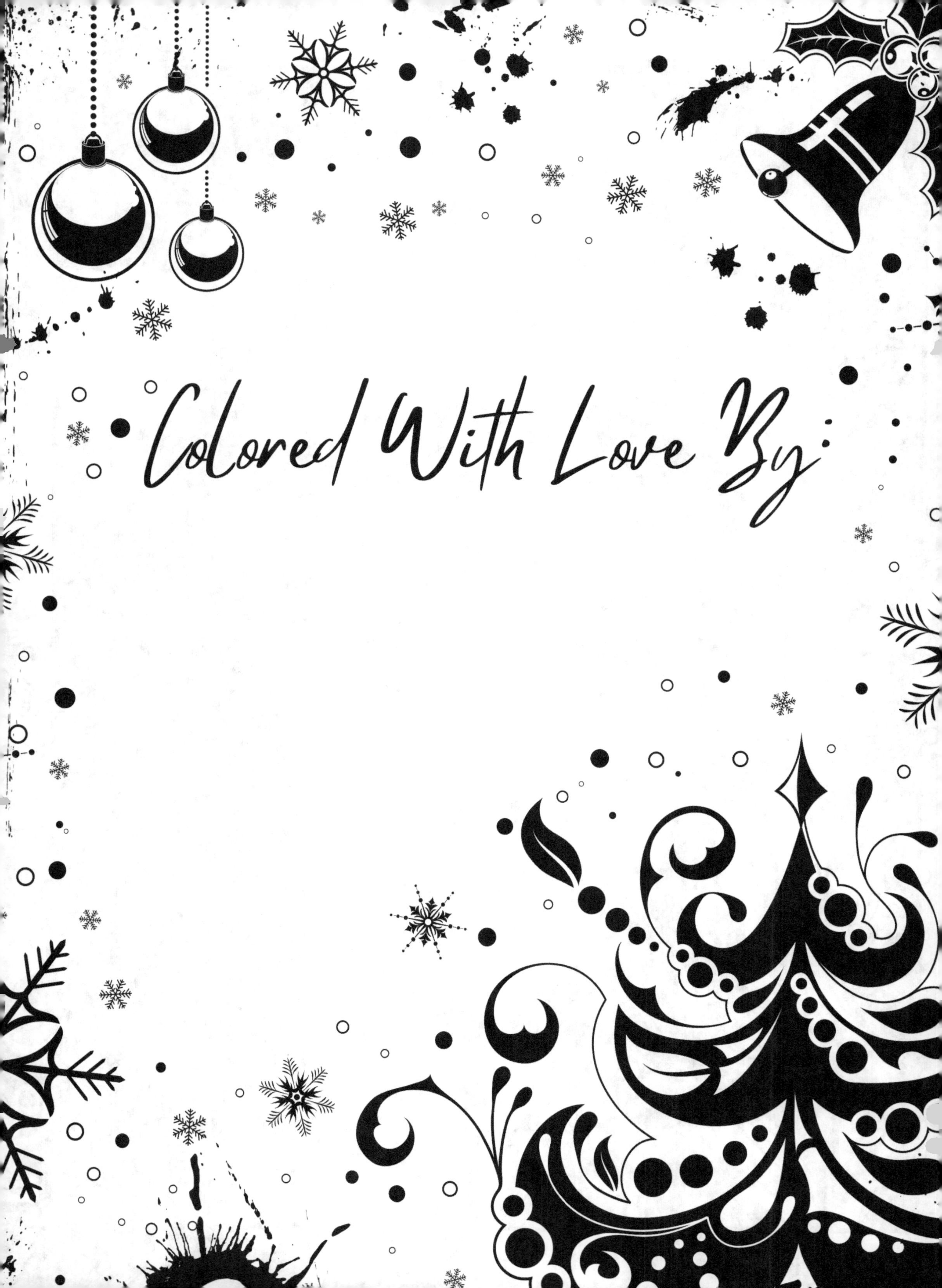
Colored With Love By:

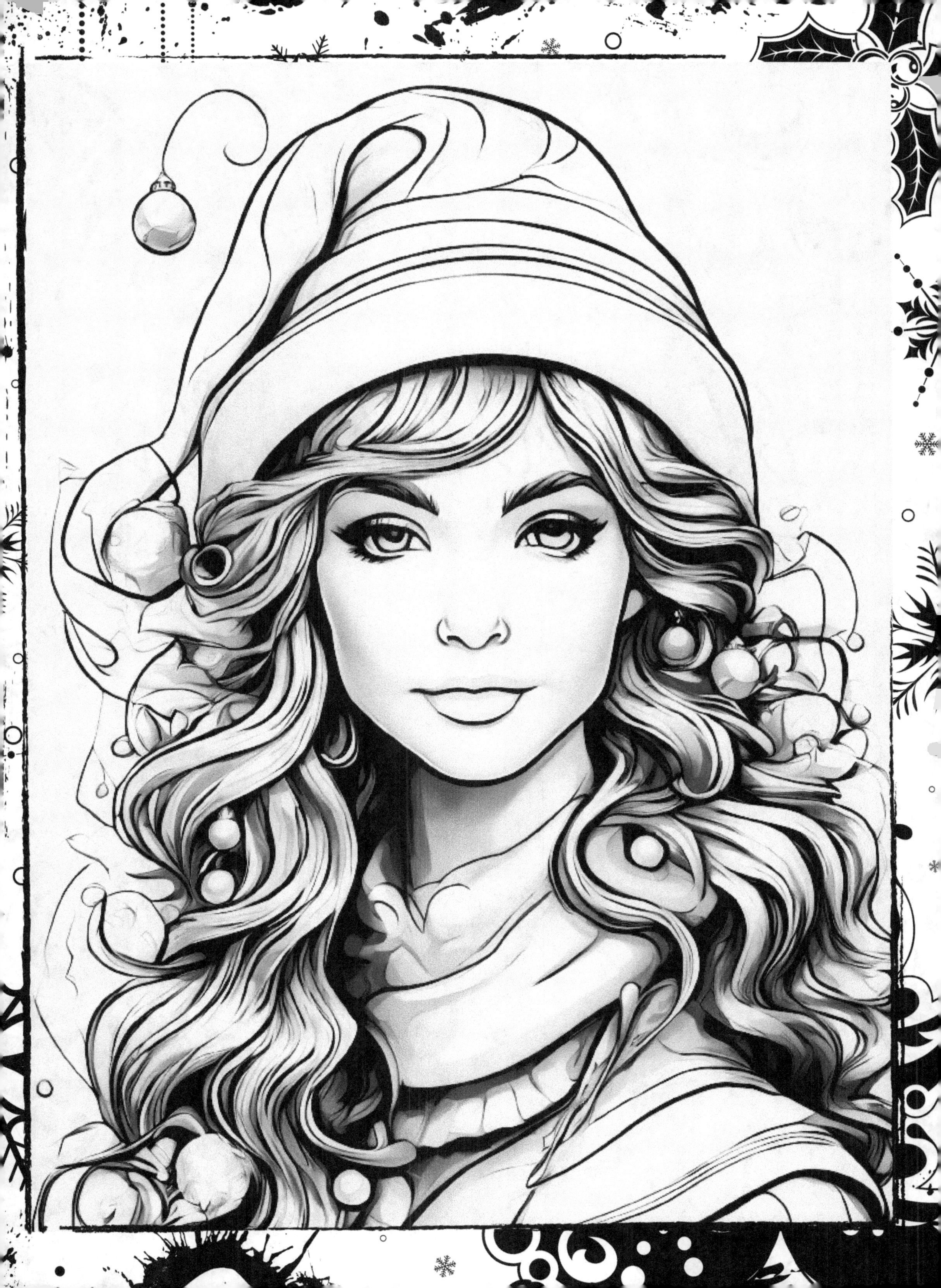

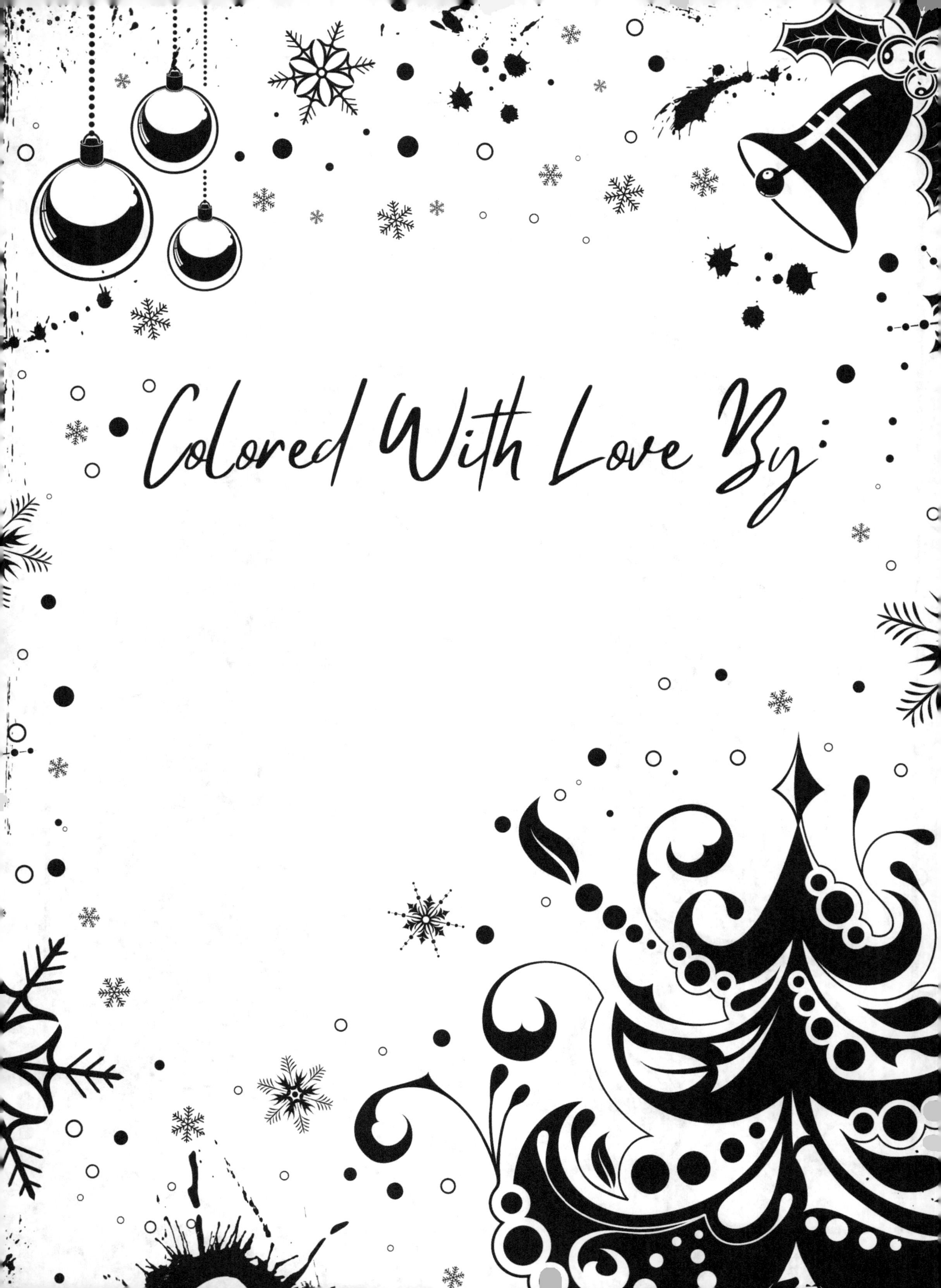
Colored With Love By:

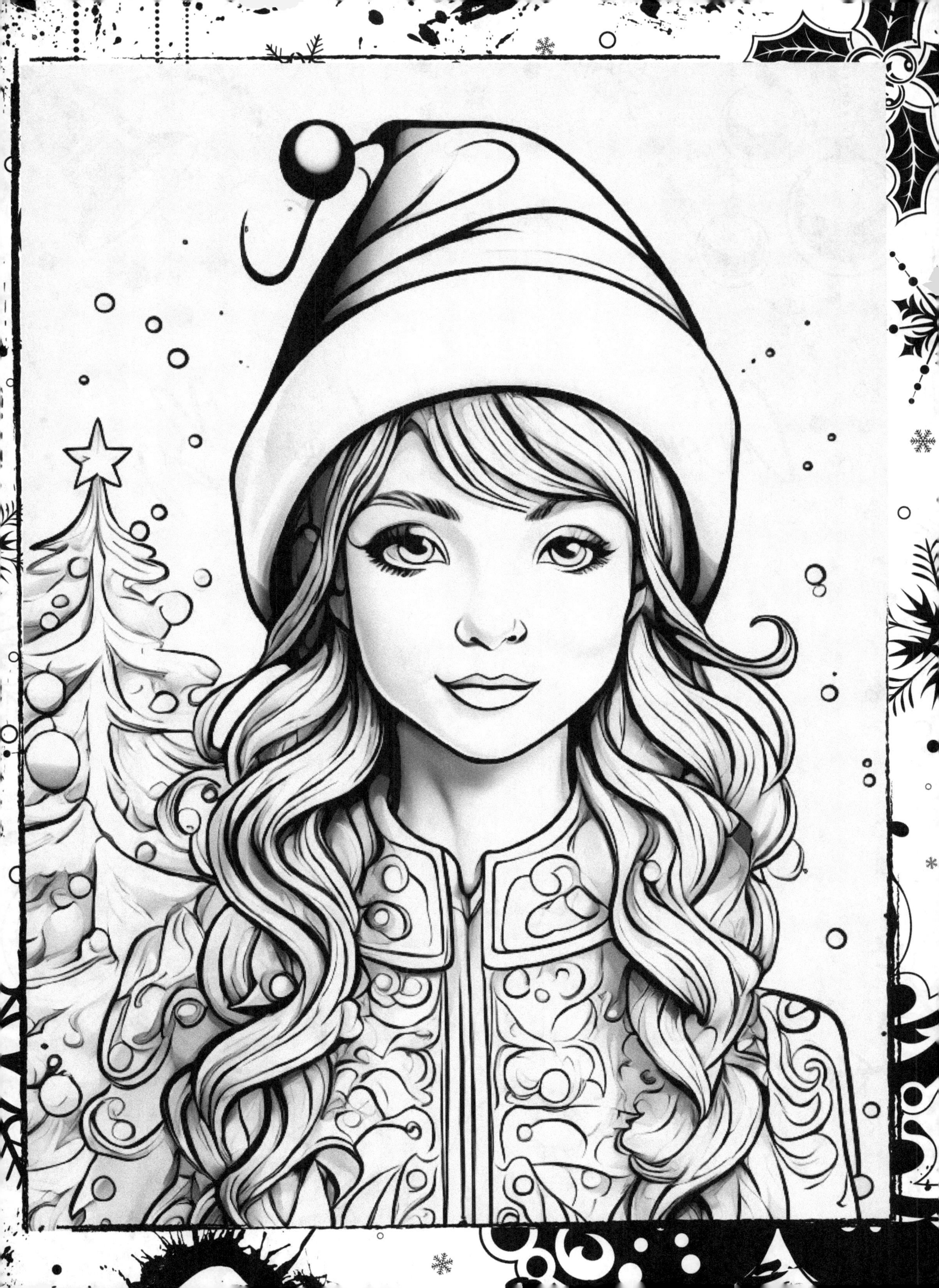

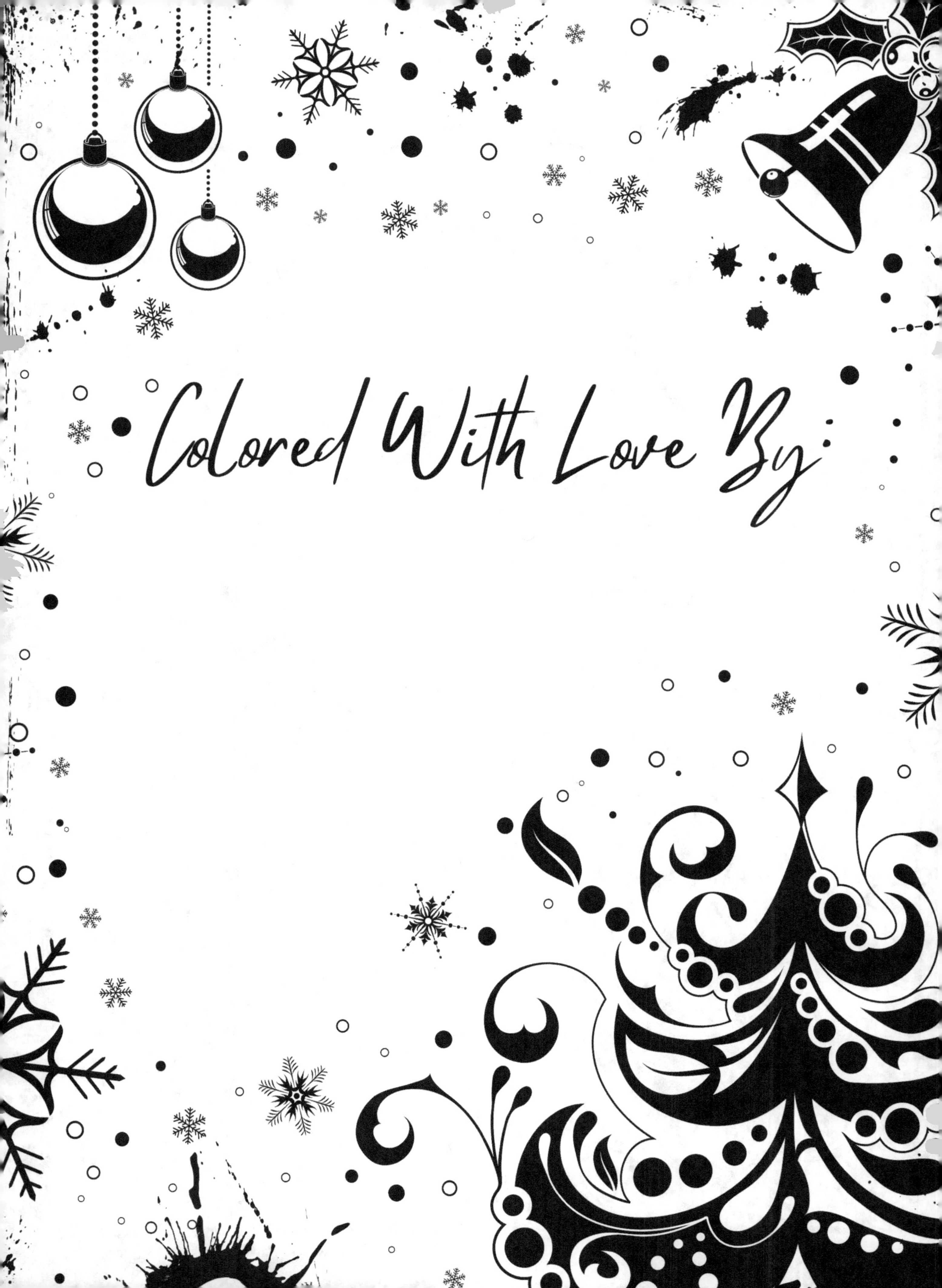
Colored With Love By:

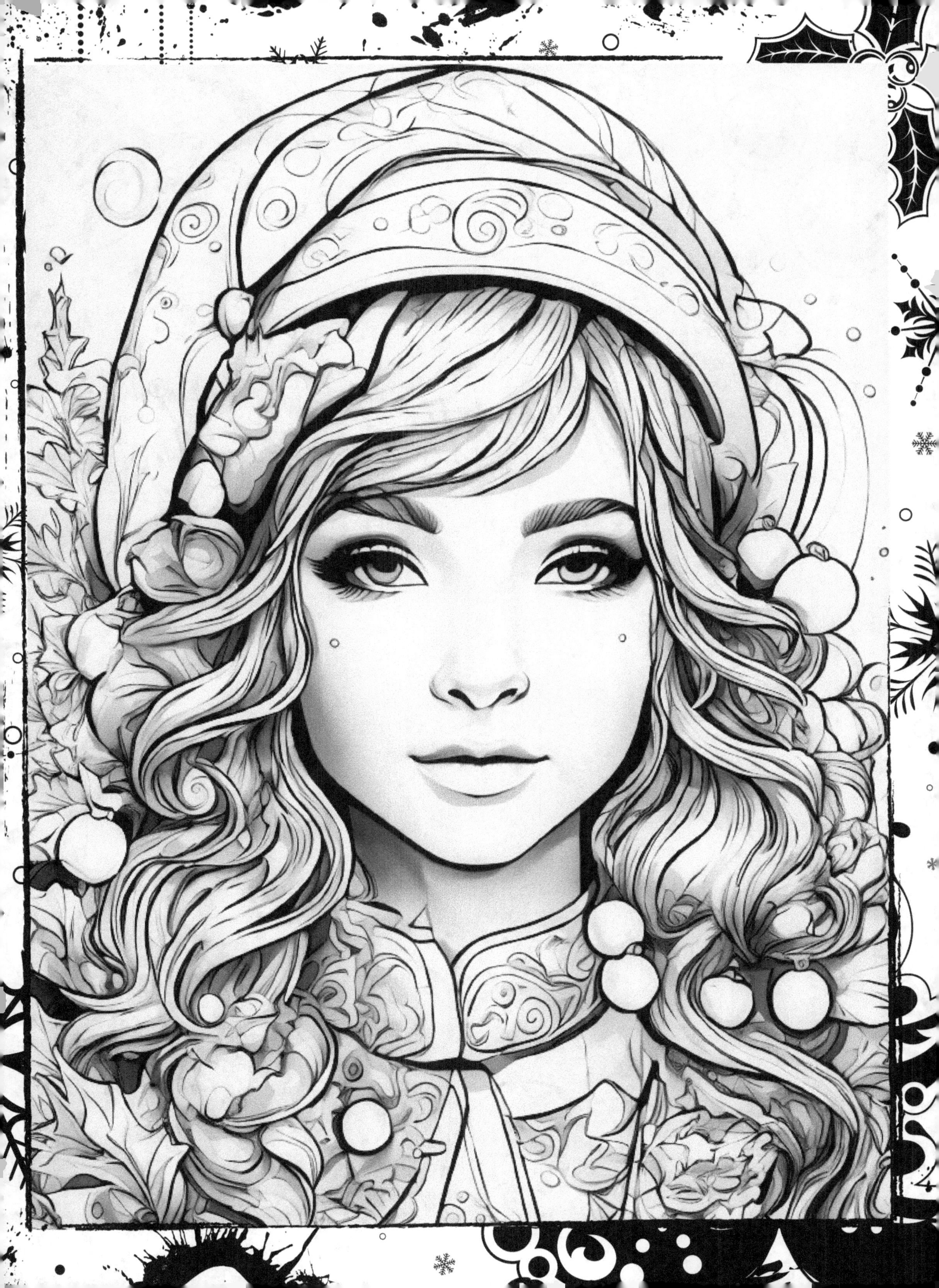

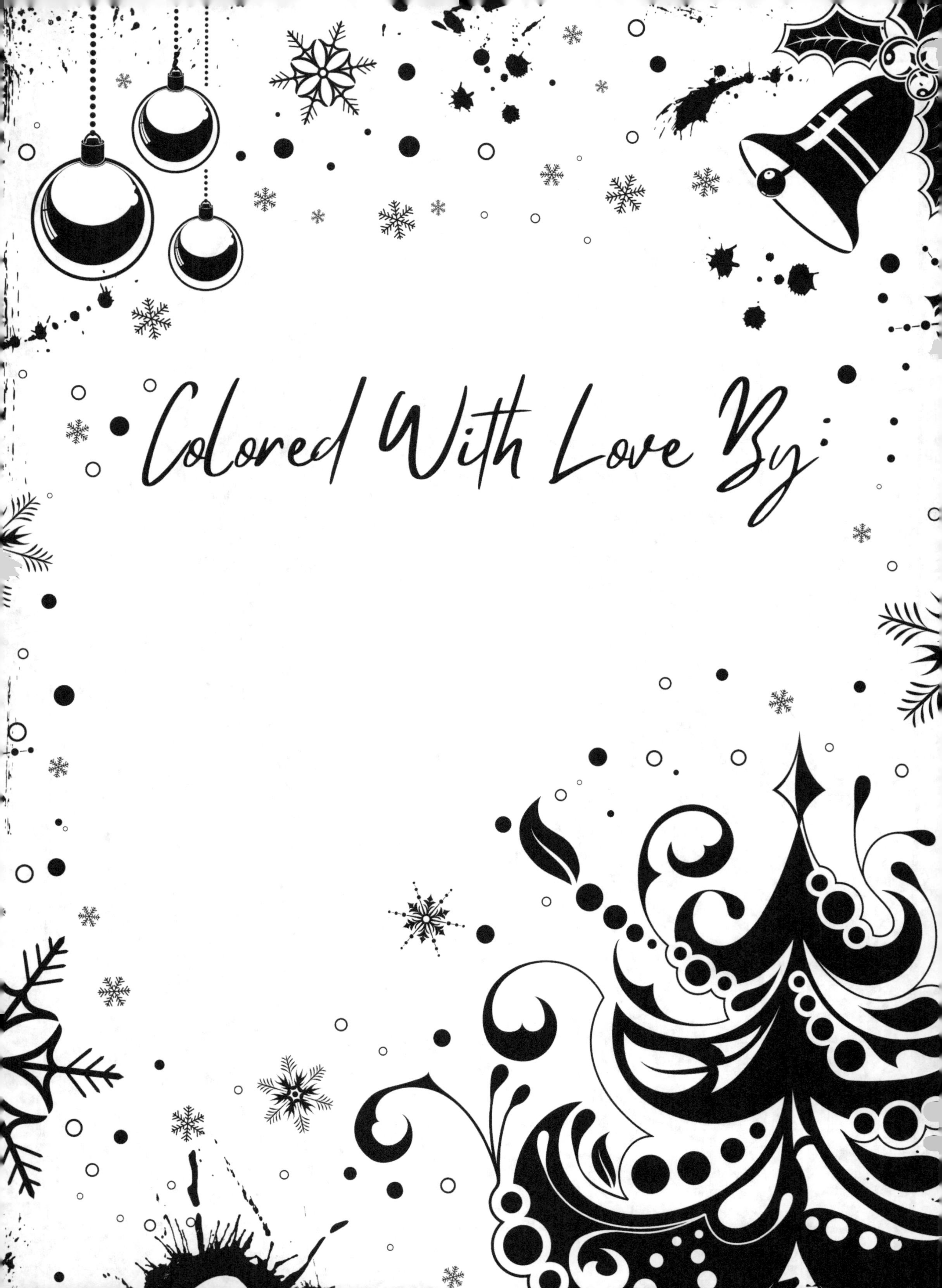
Colored With Love By:

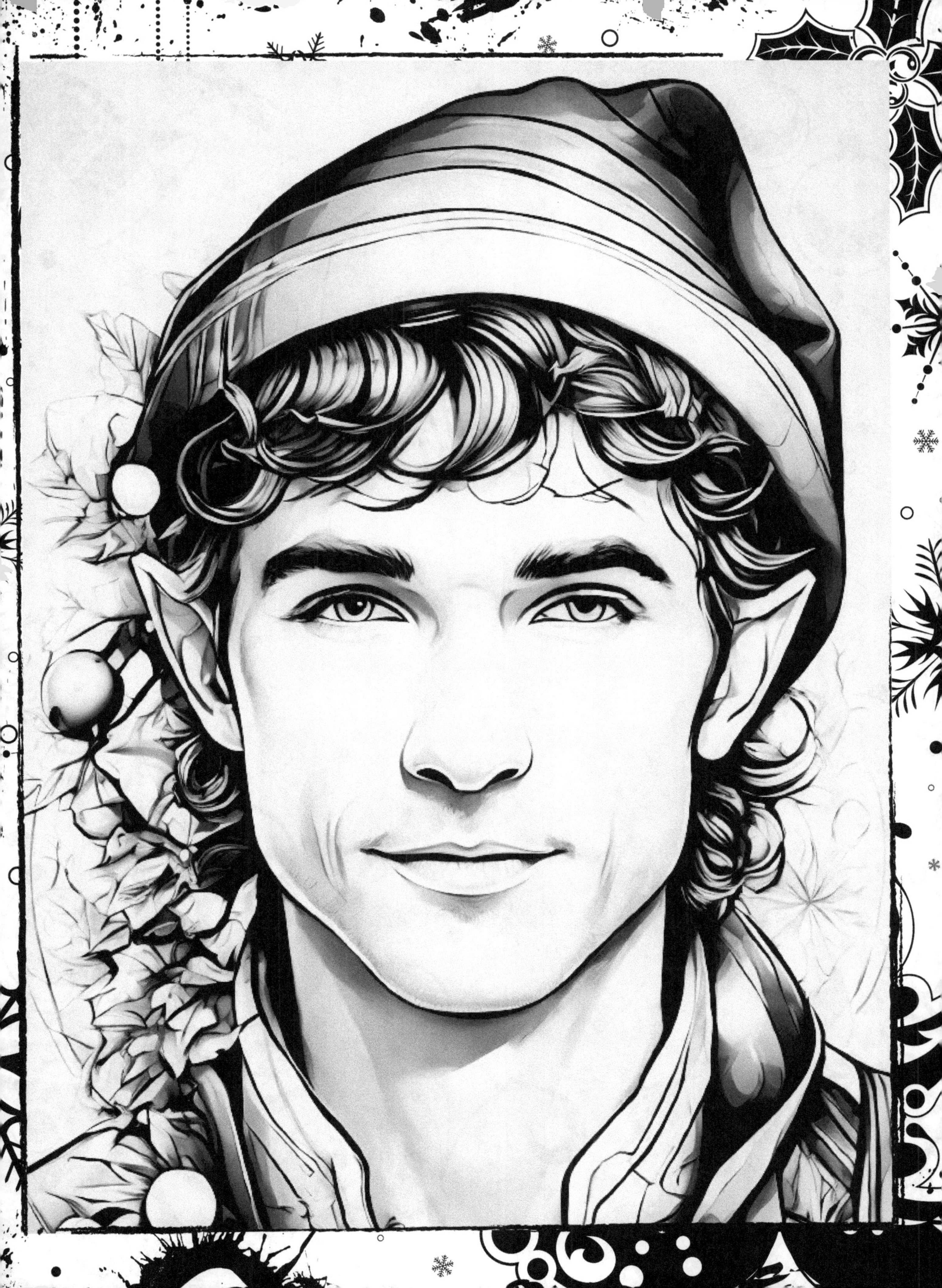

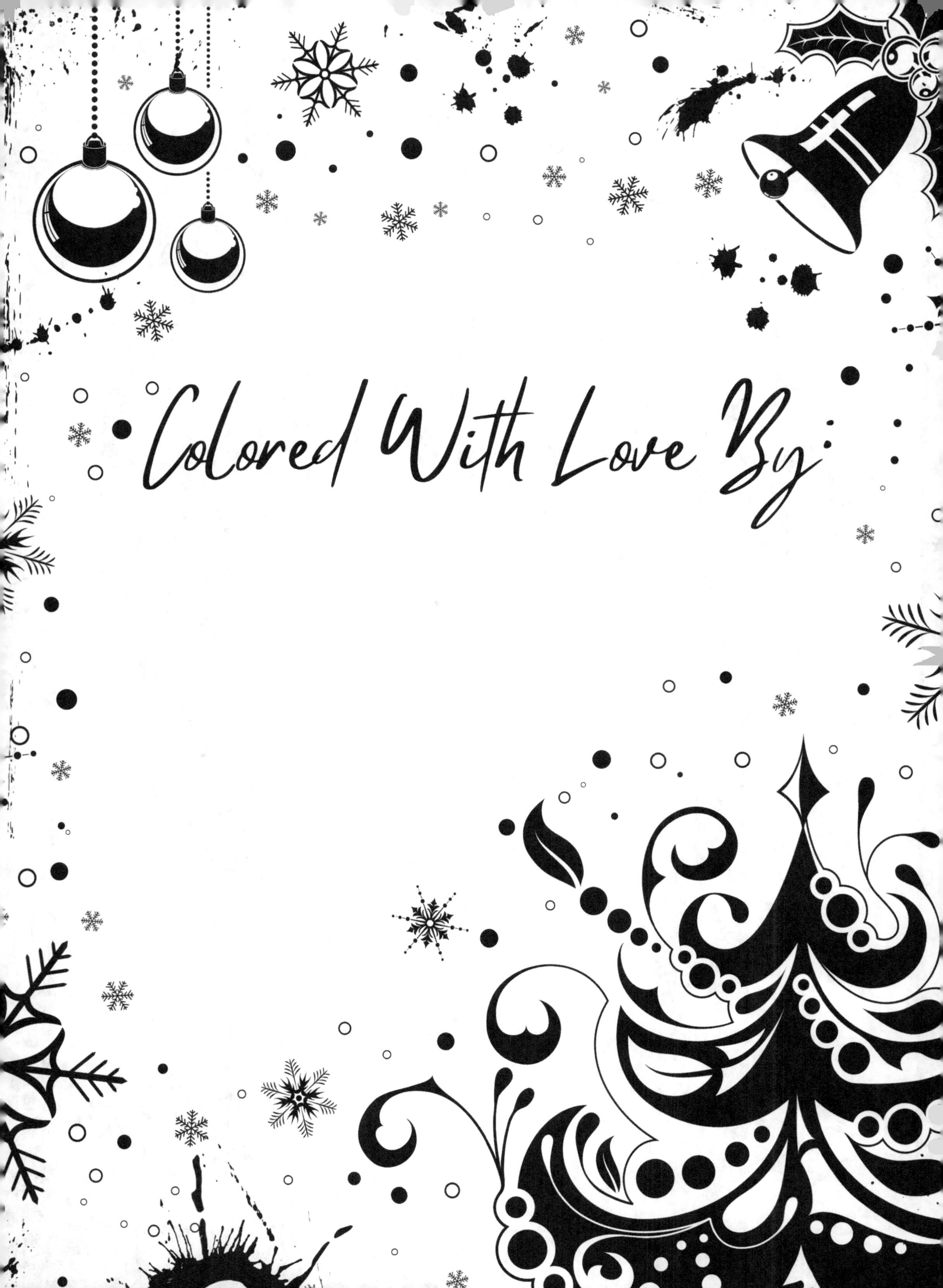

Colored With Love By:

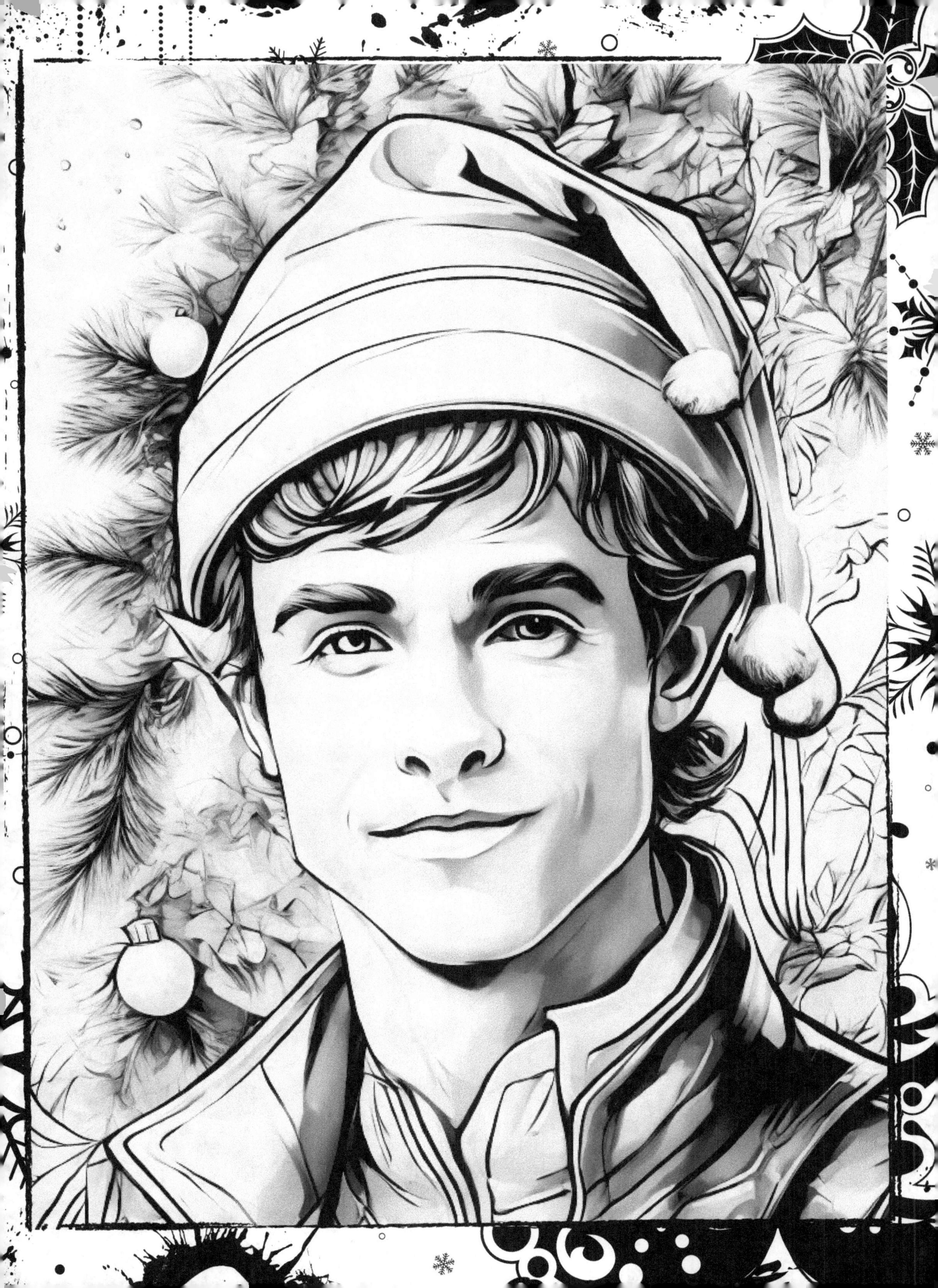

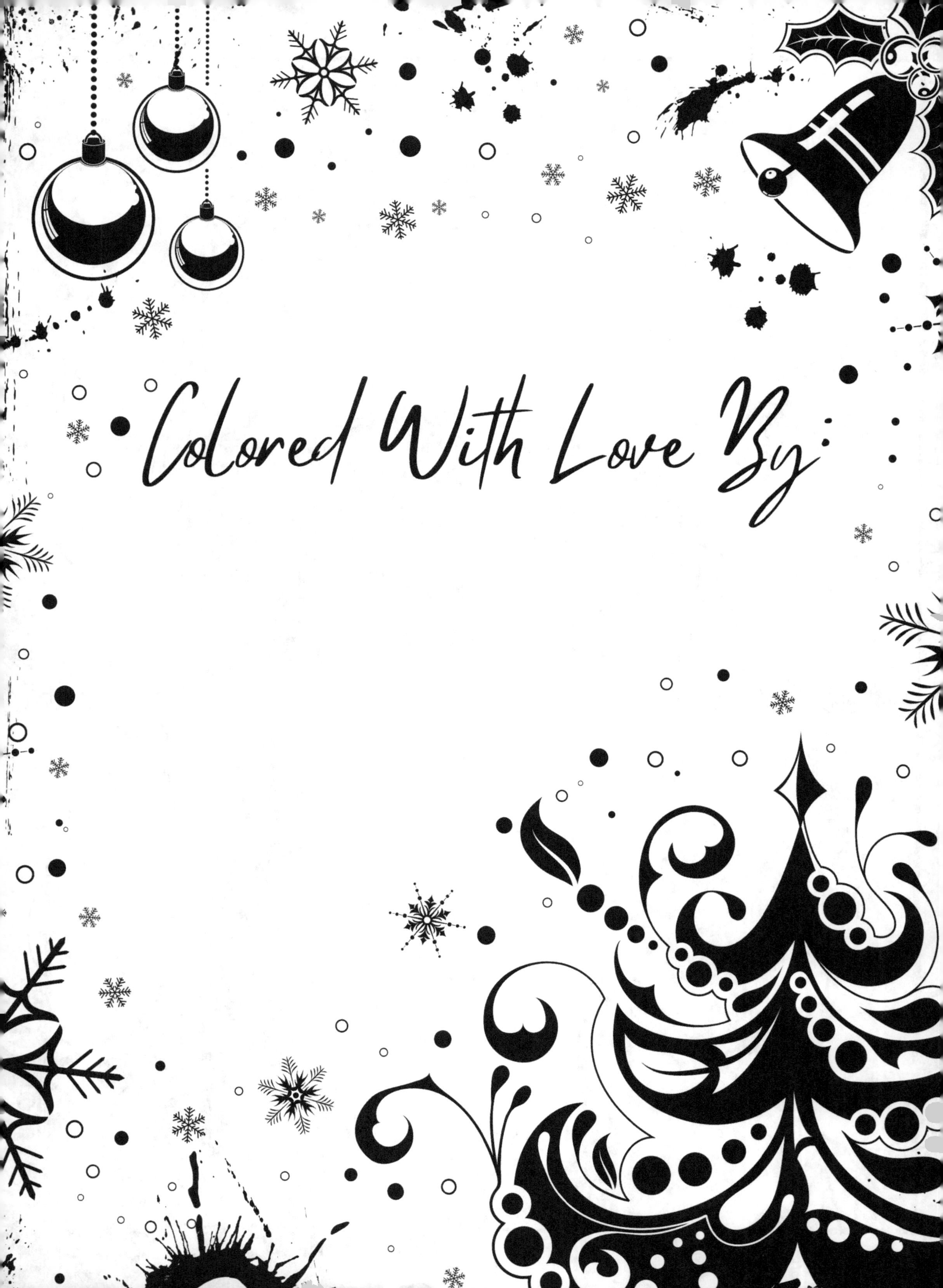
Colored With Love By:

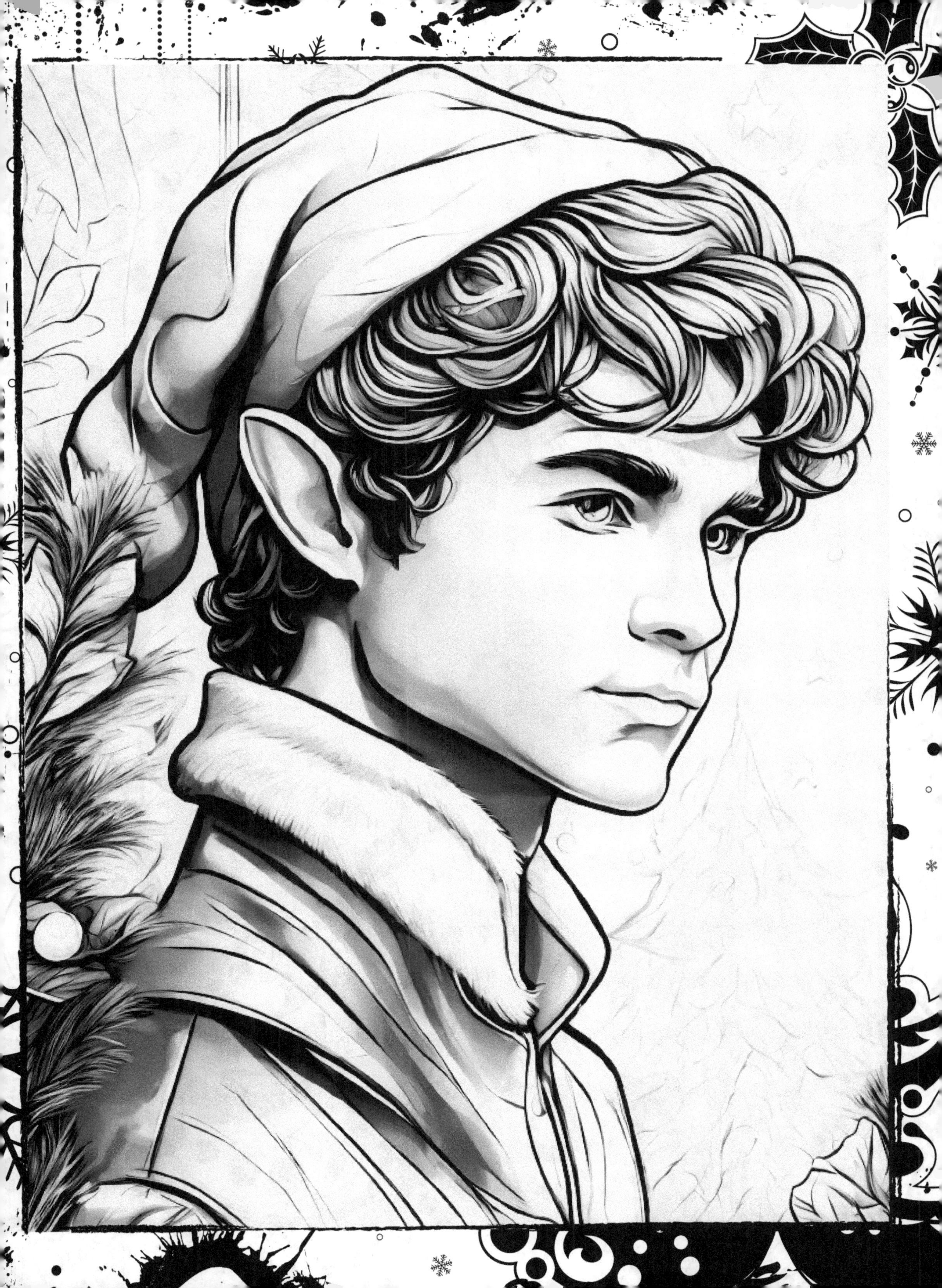

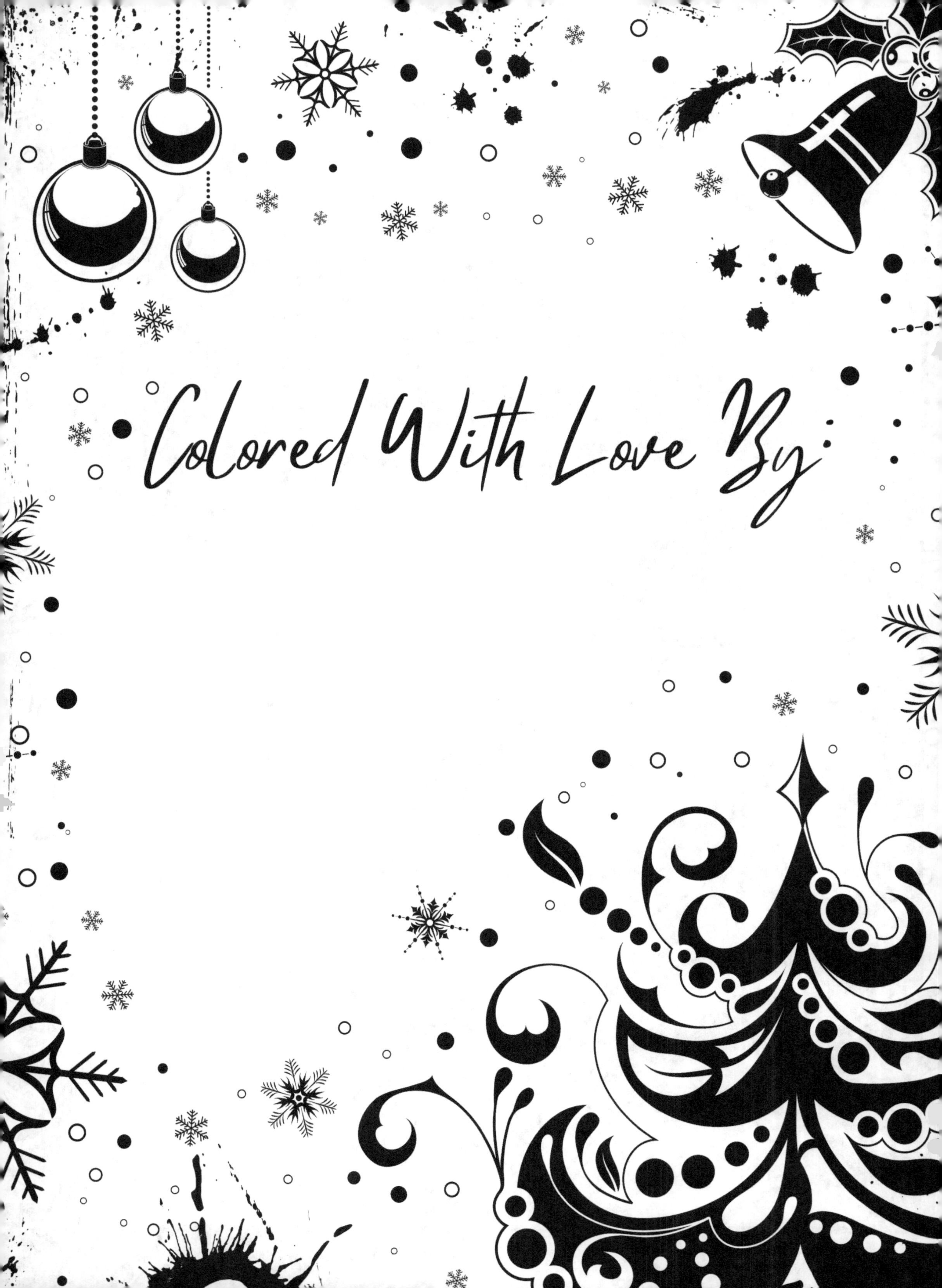

Colored With Love By:

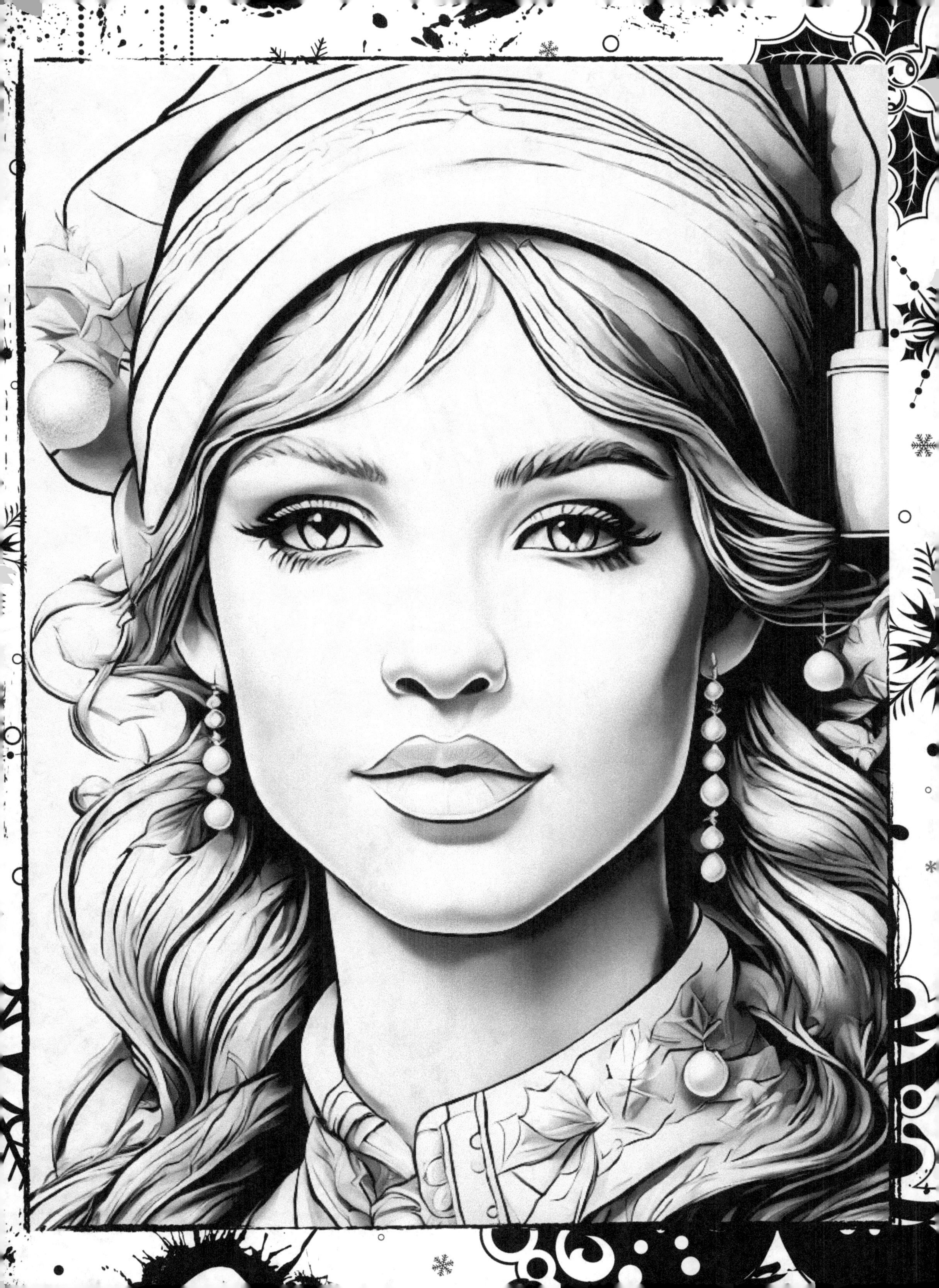

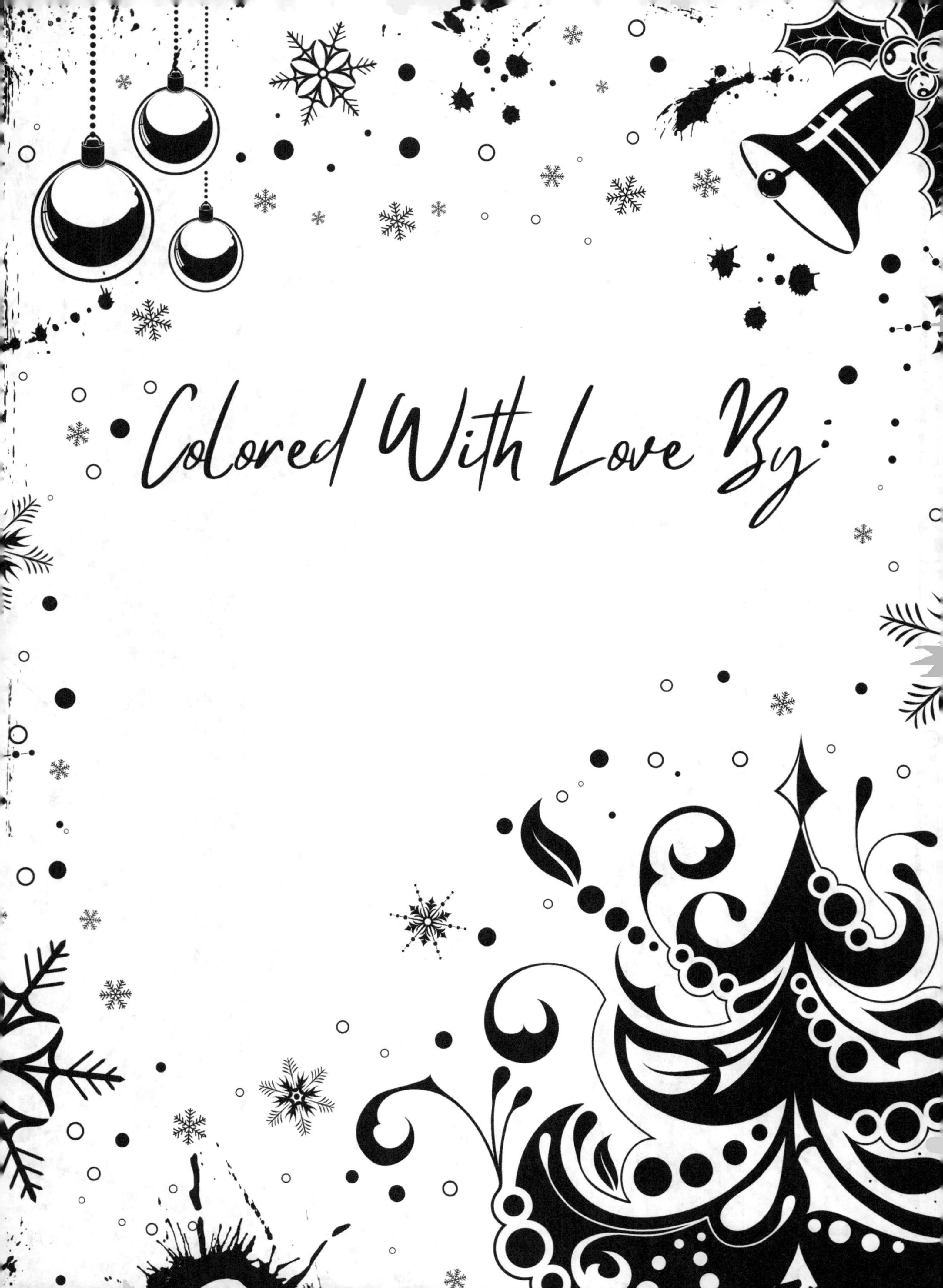

Colored With Love By:

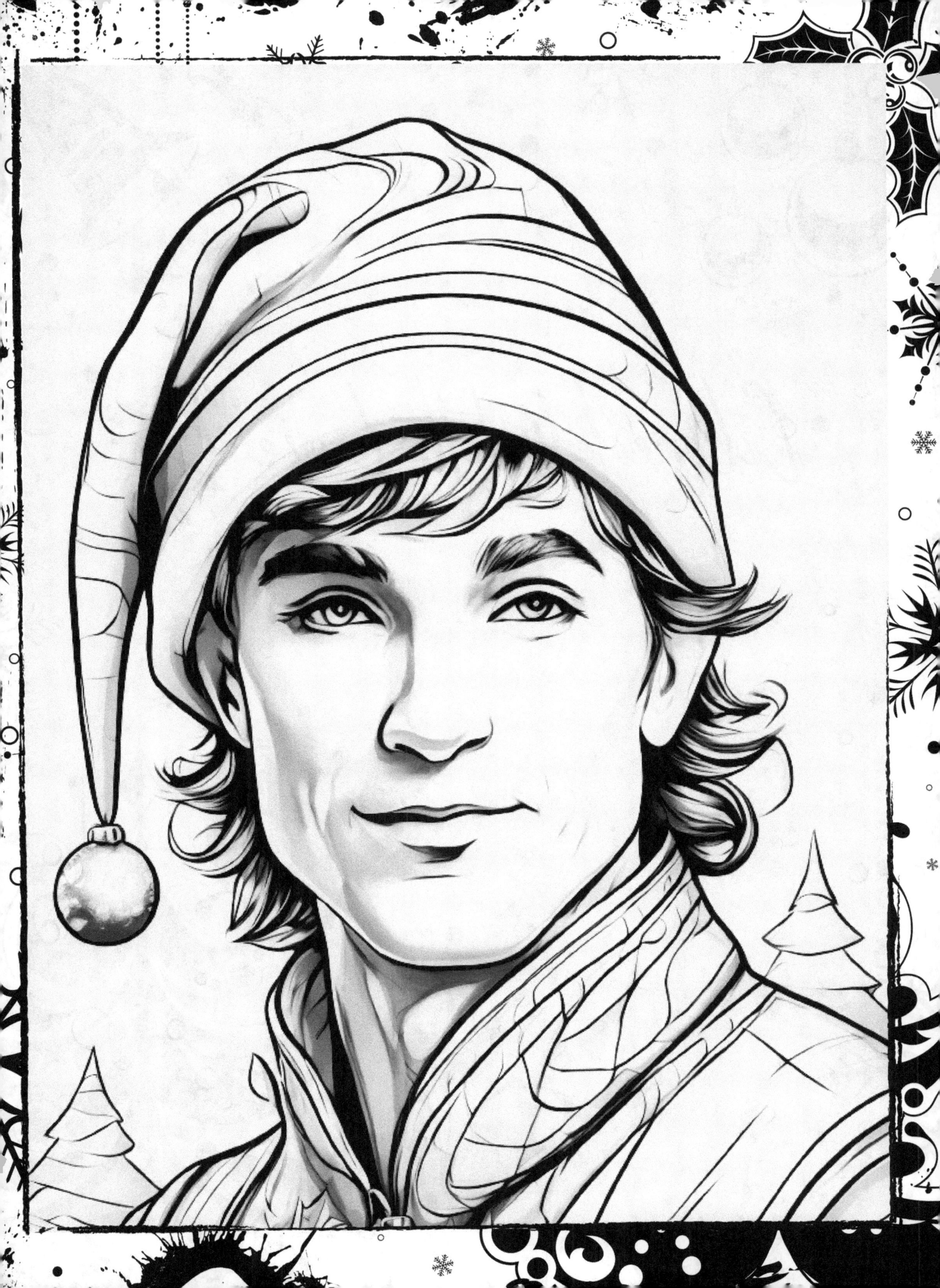

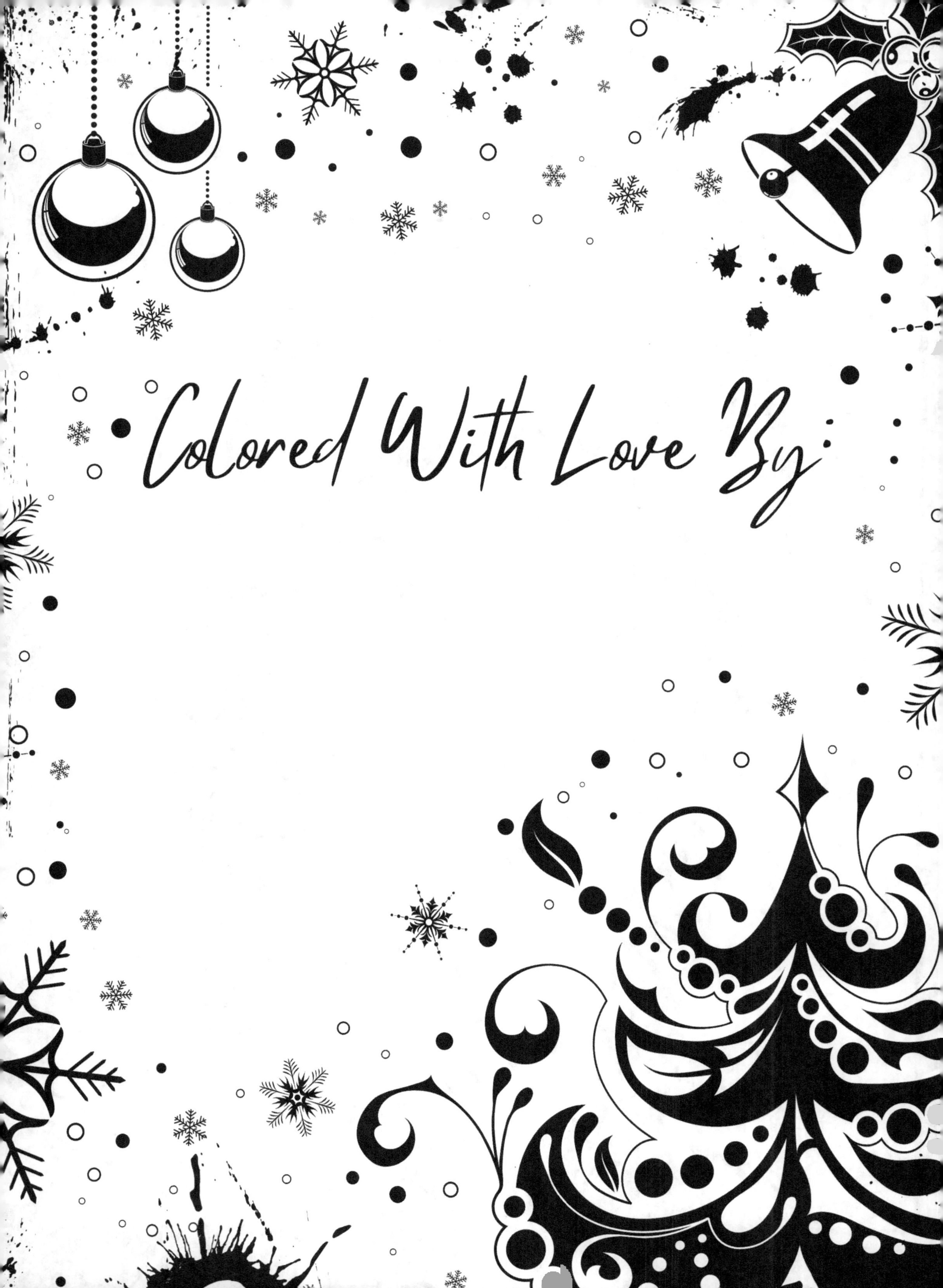

Colored With Love By:

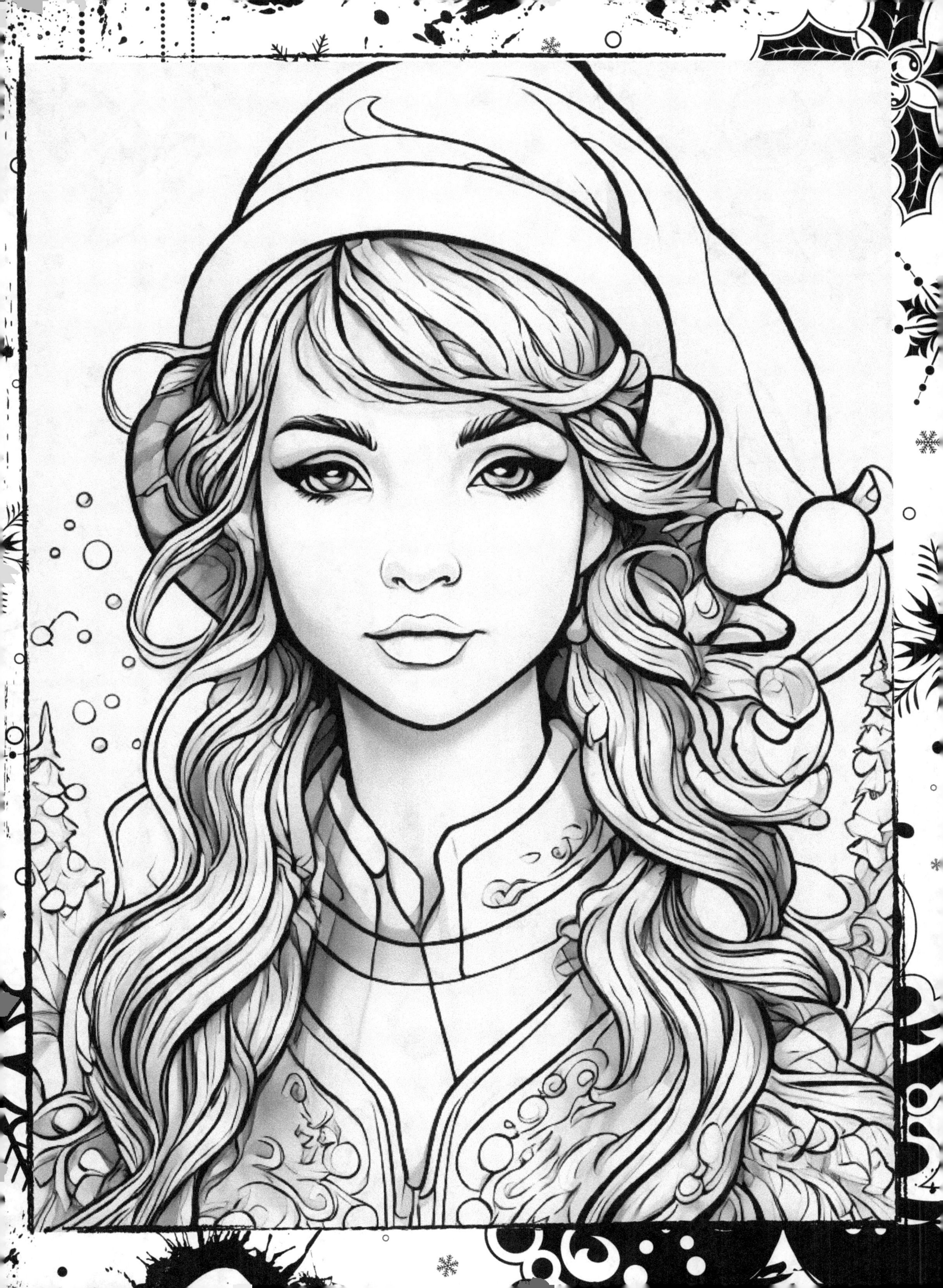

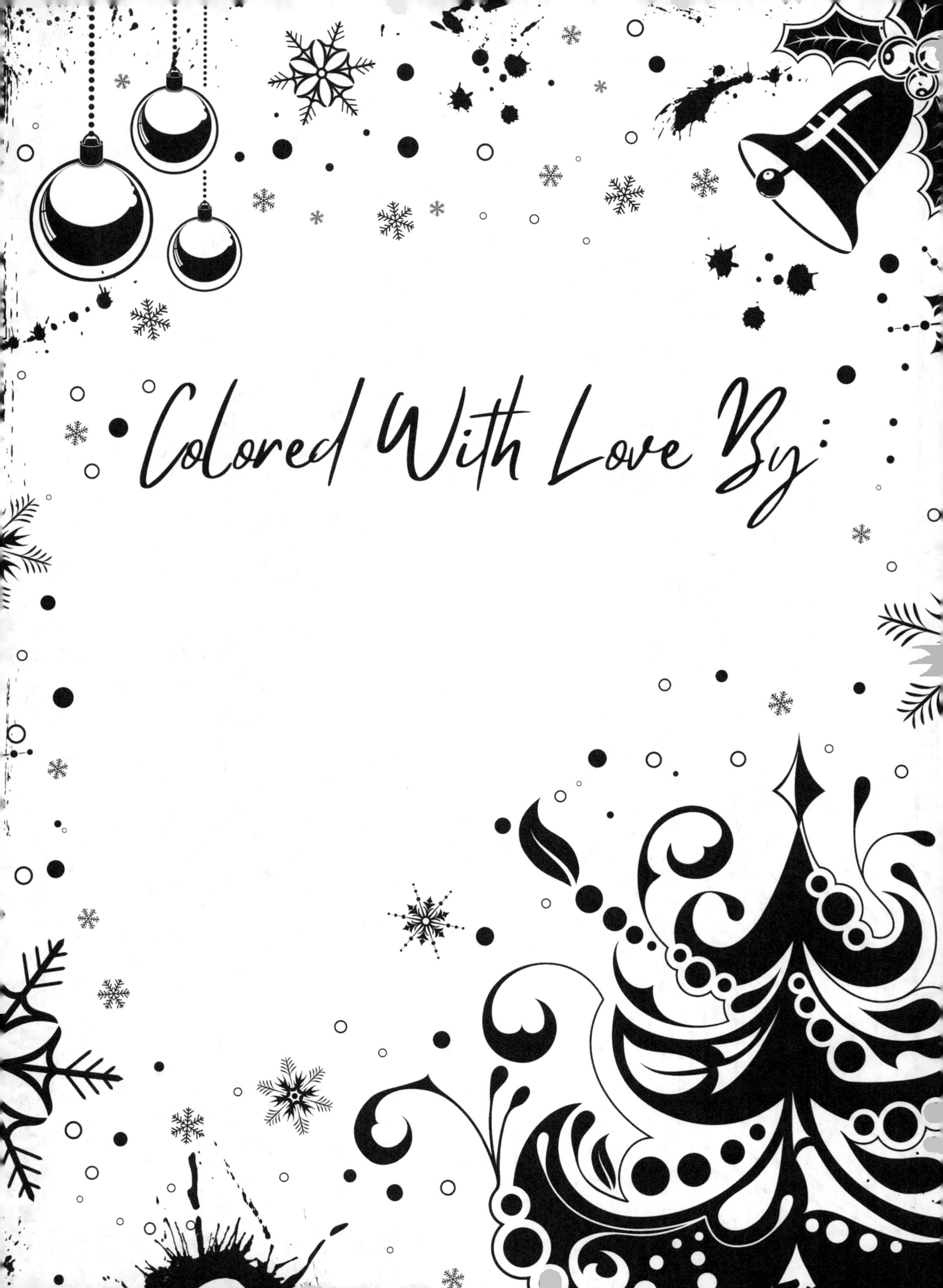
Colored With Love By:

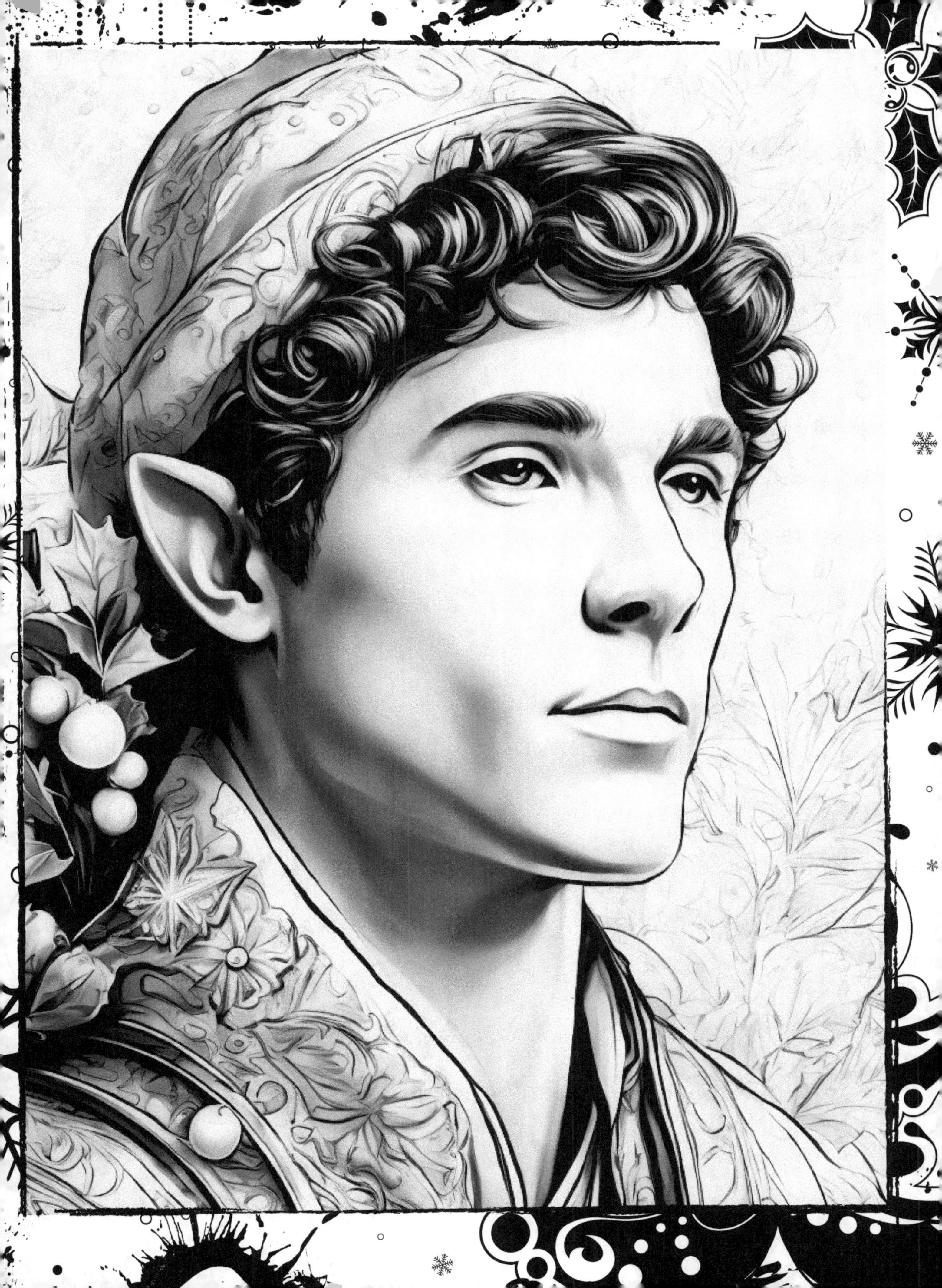

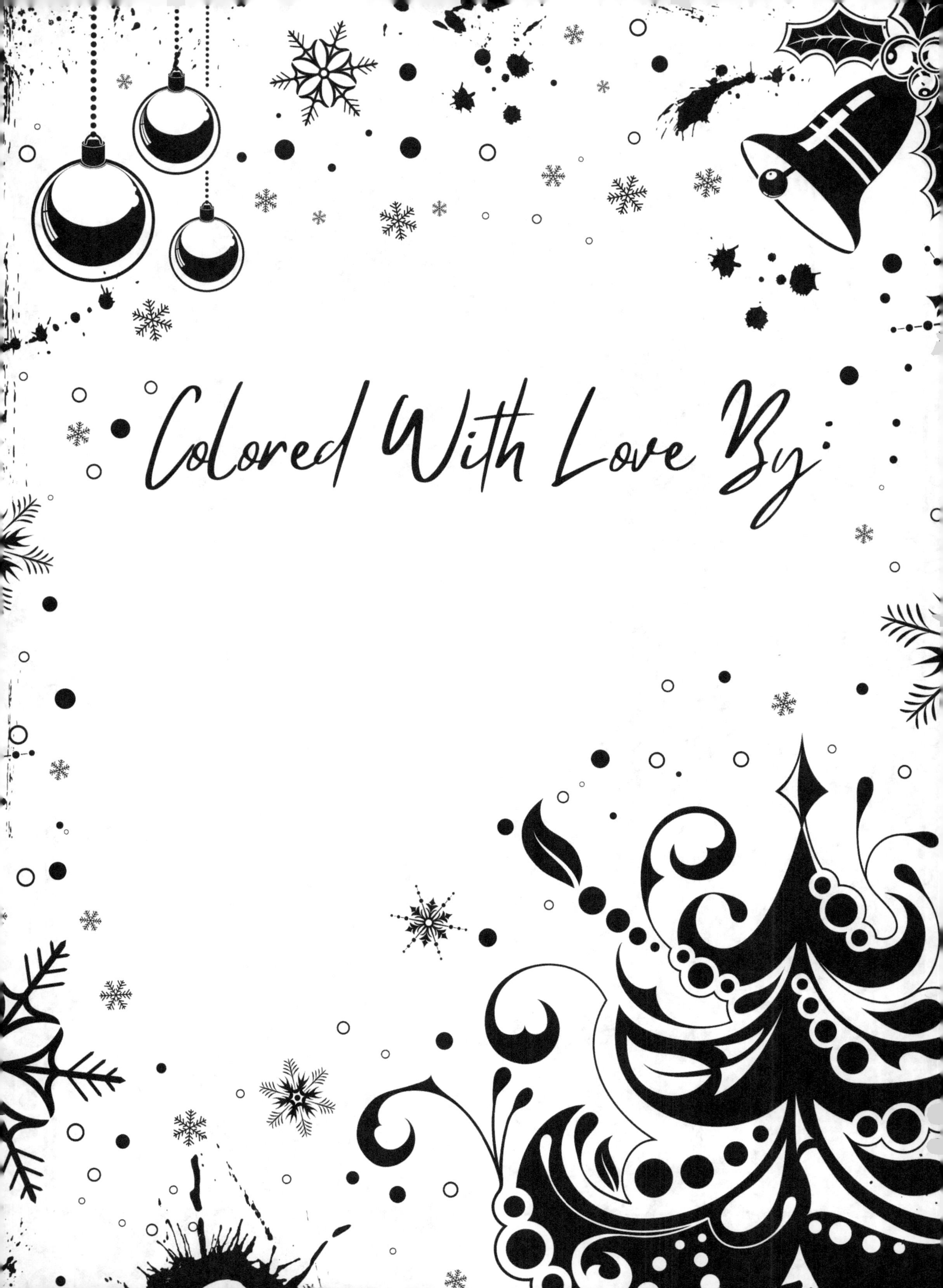
Colored With Love By:

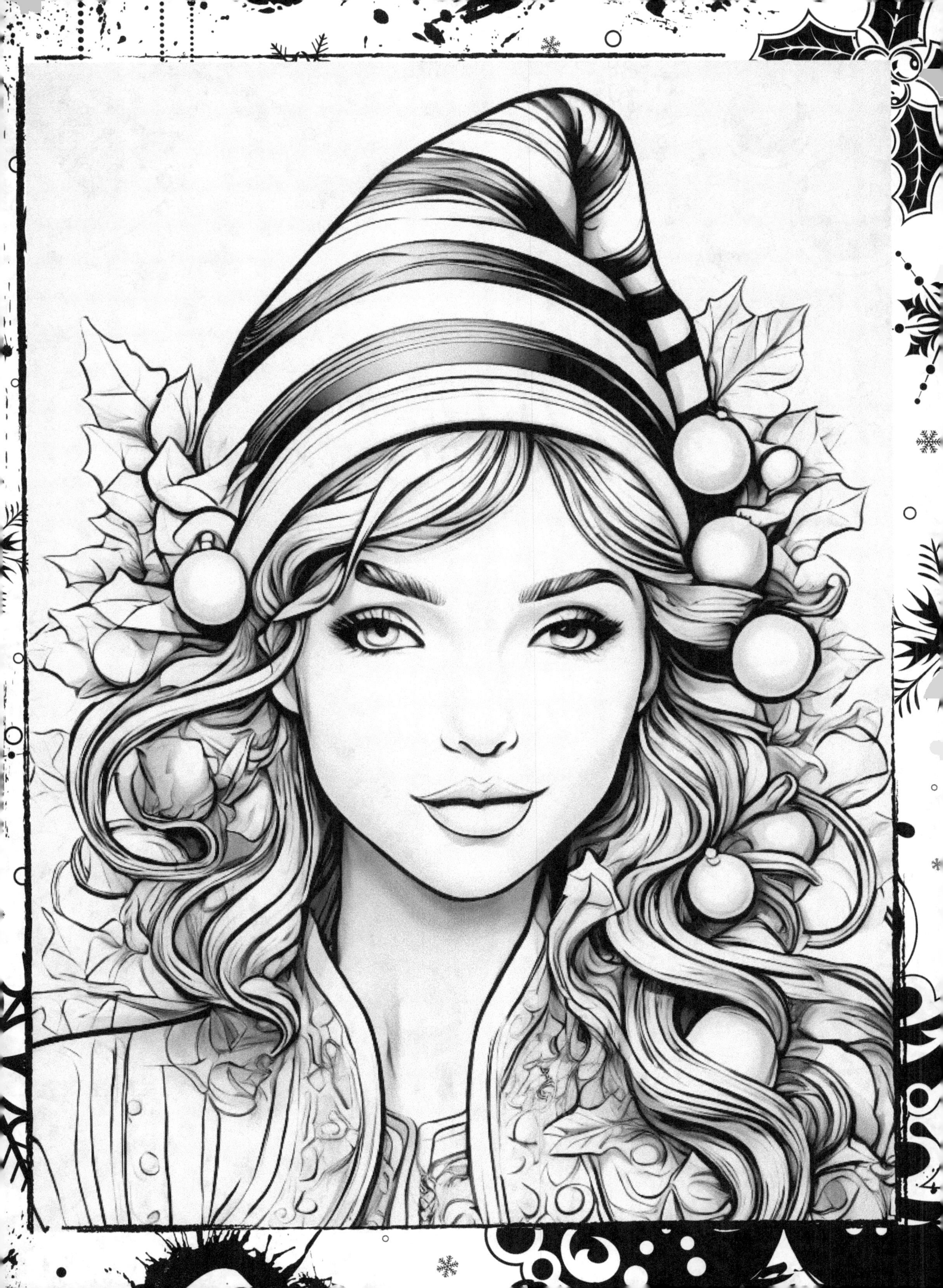

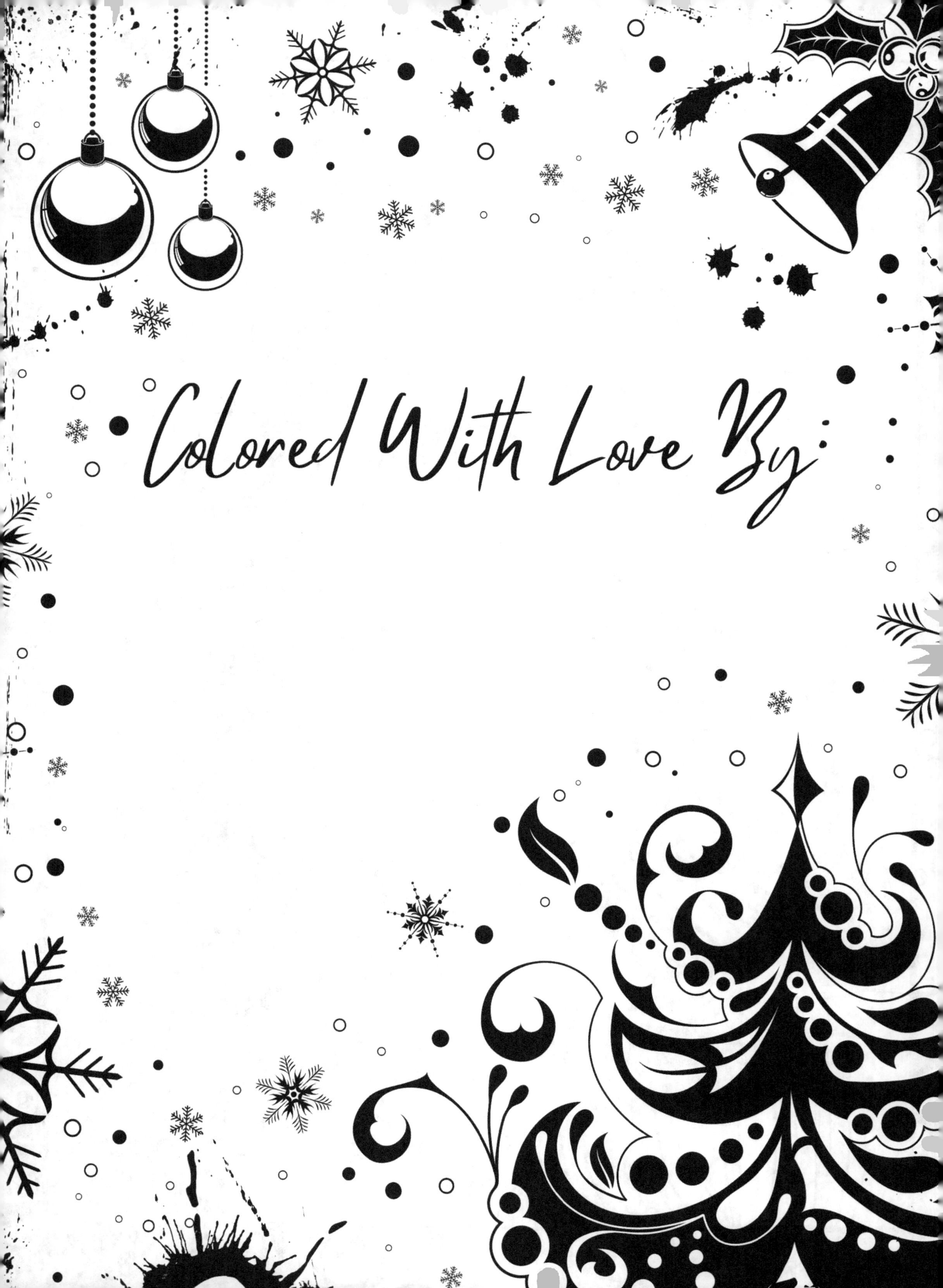
Colored With Love By:

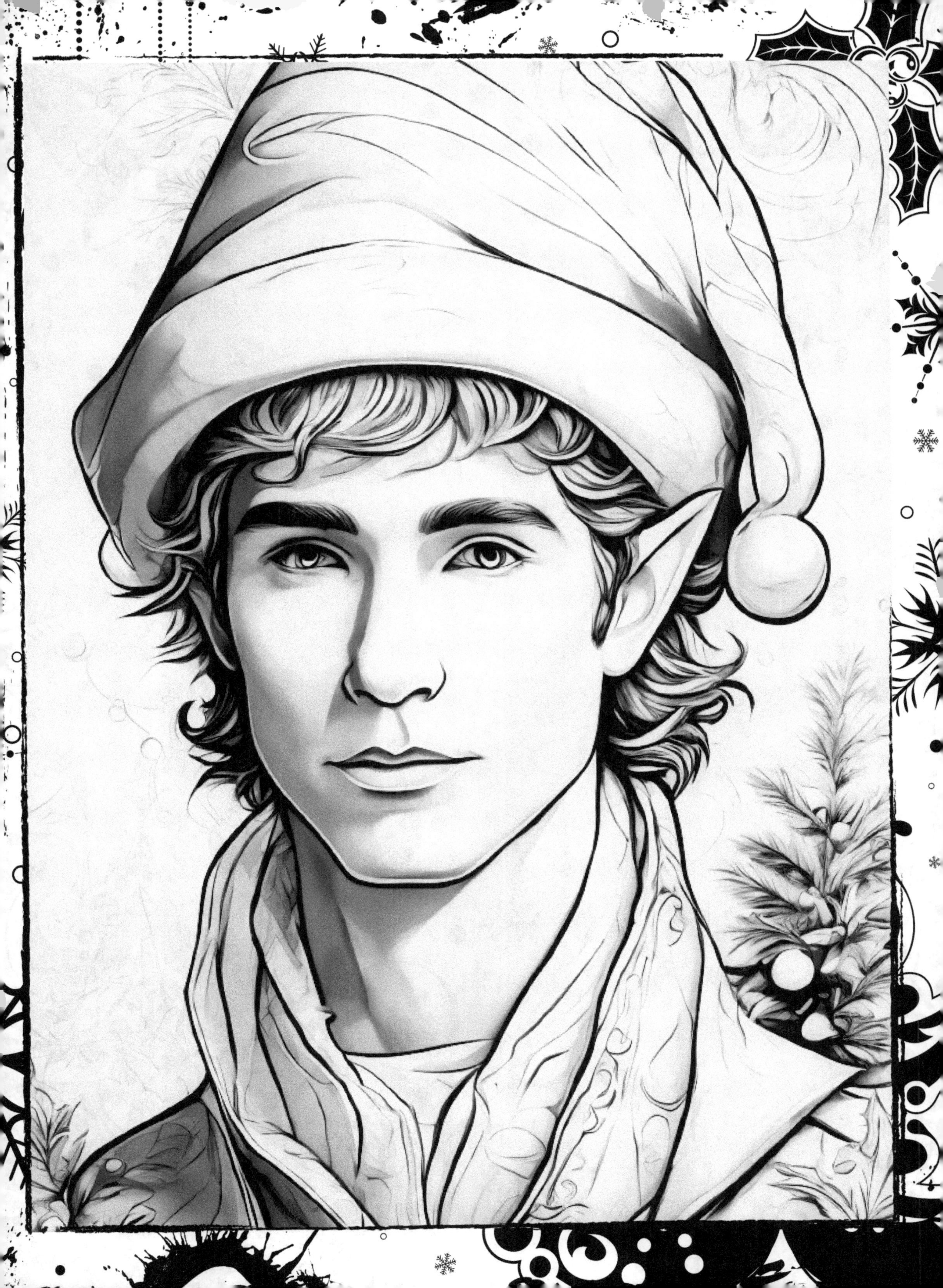

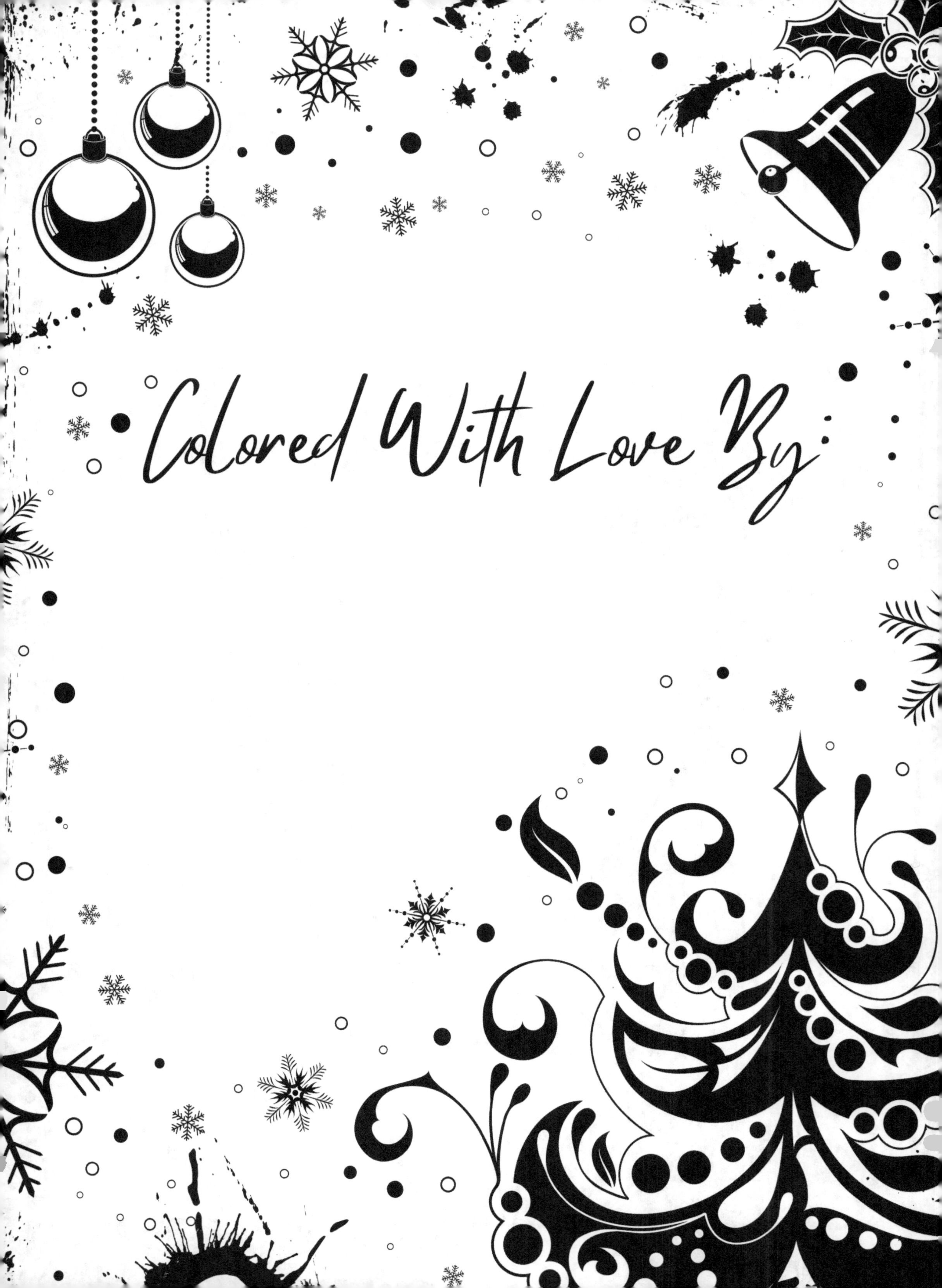
Colored With Love By:

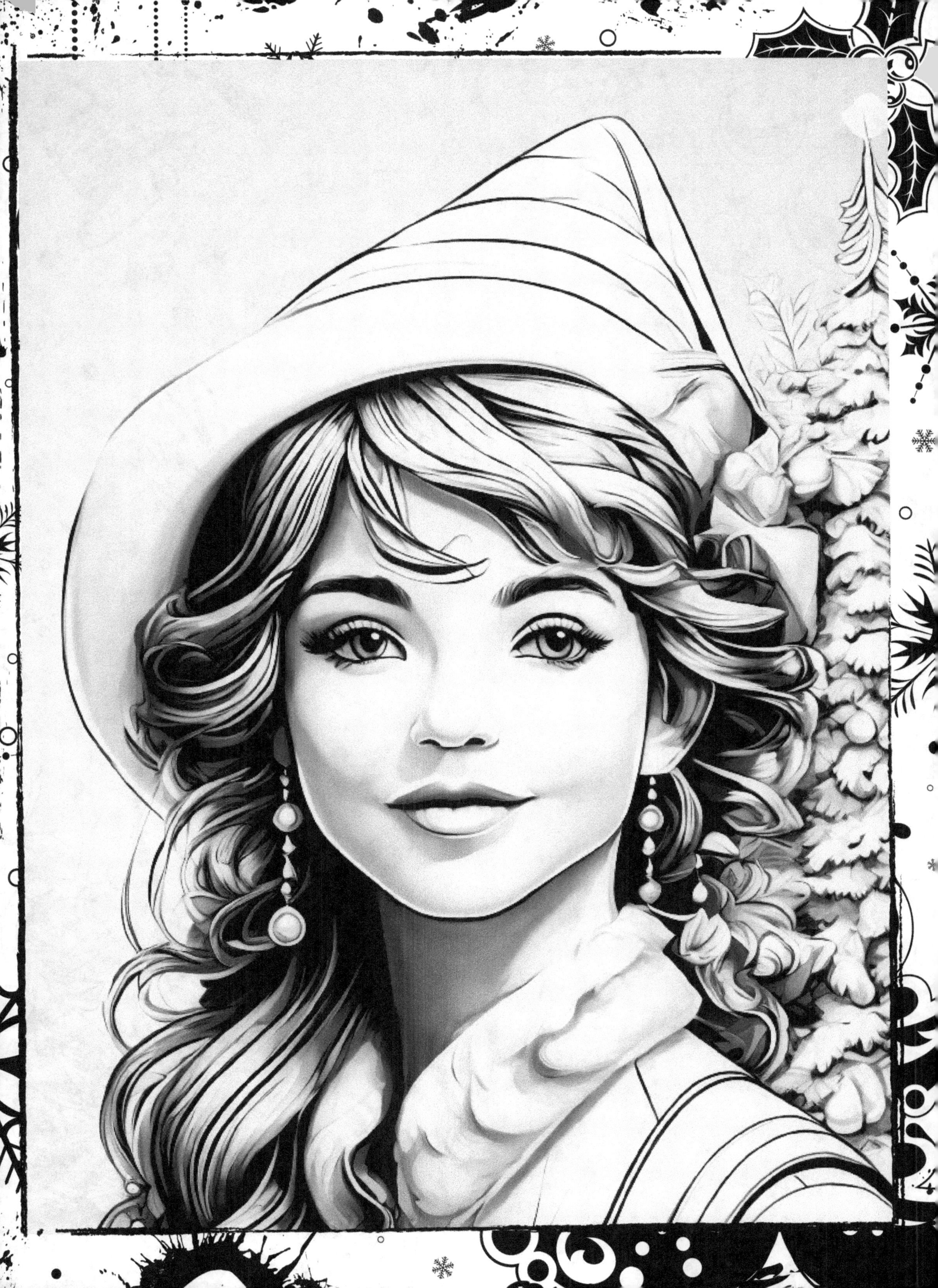

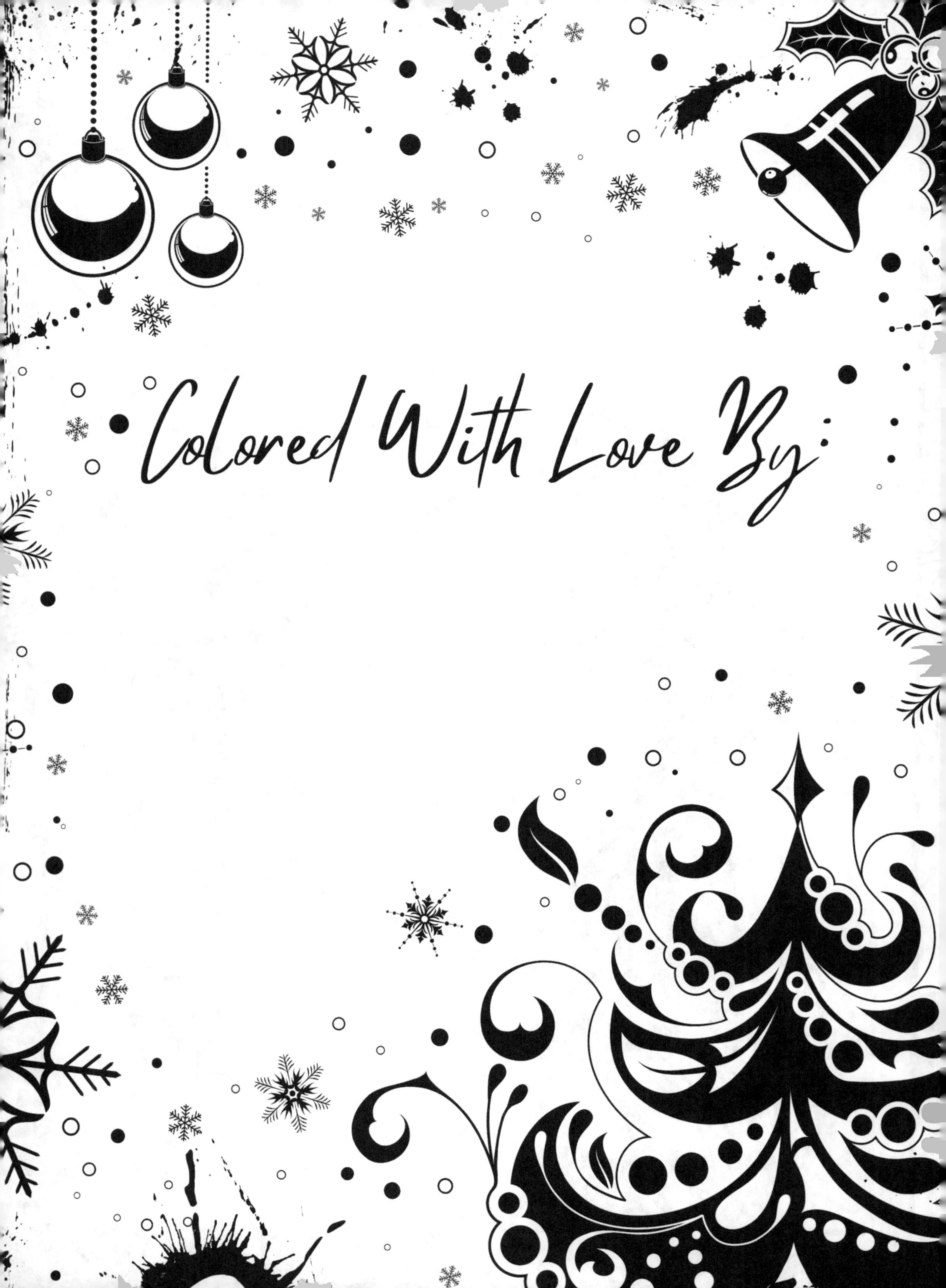

Colored With Love By:

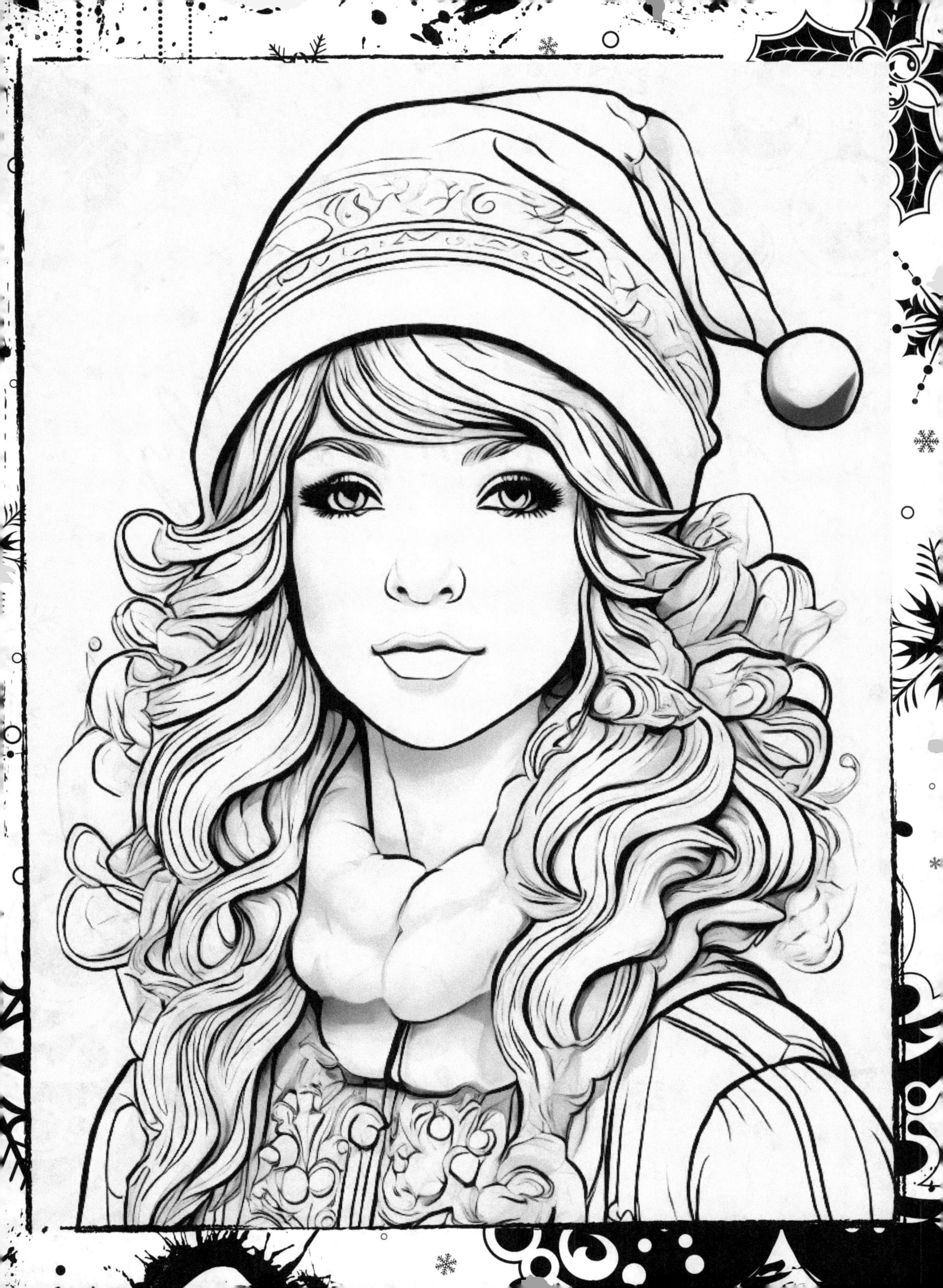

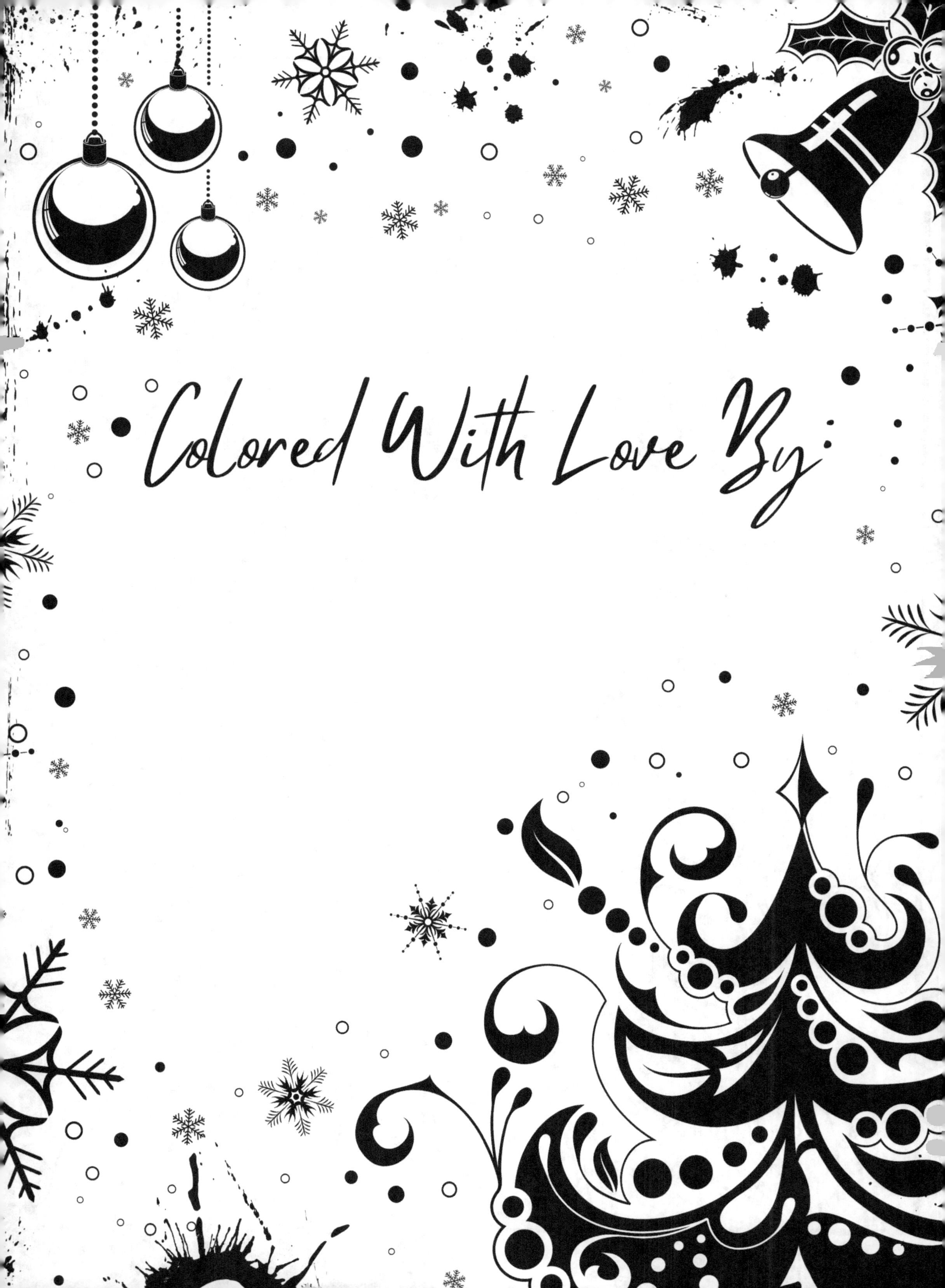

Colored With Love By:

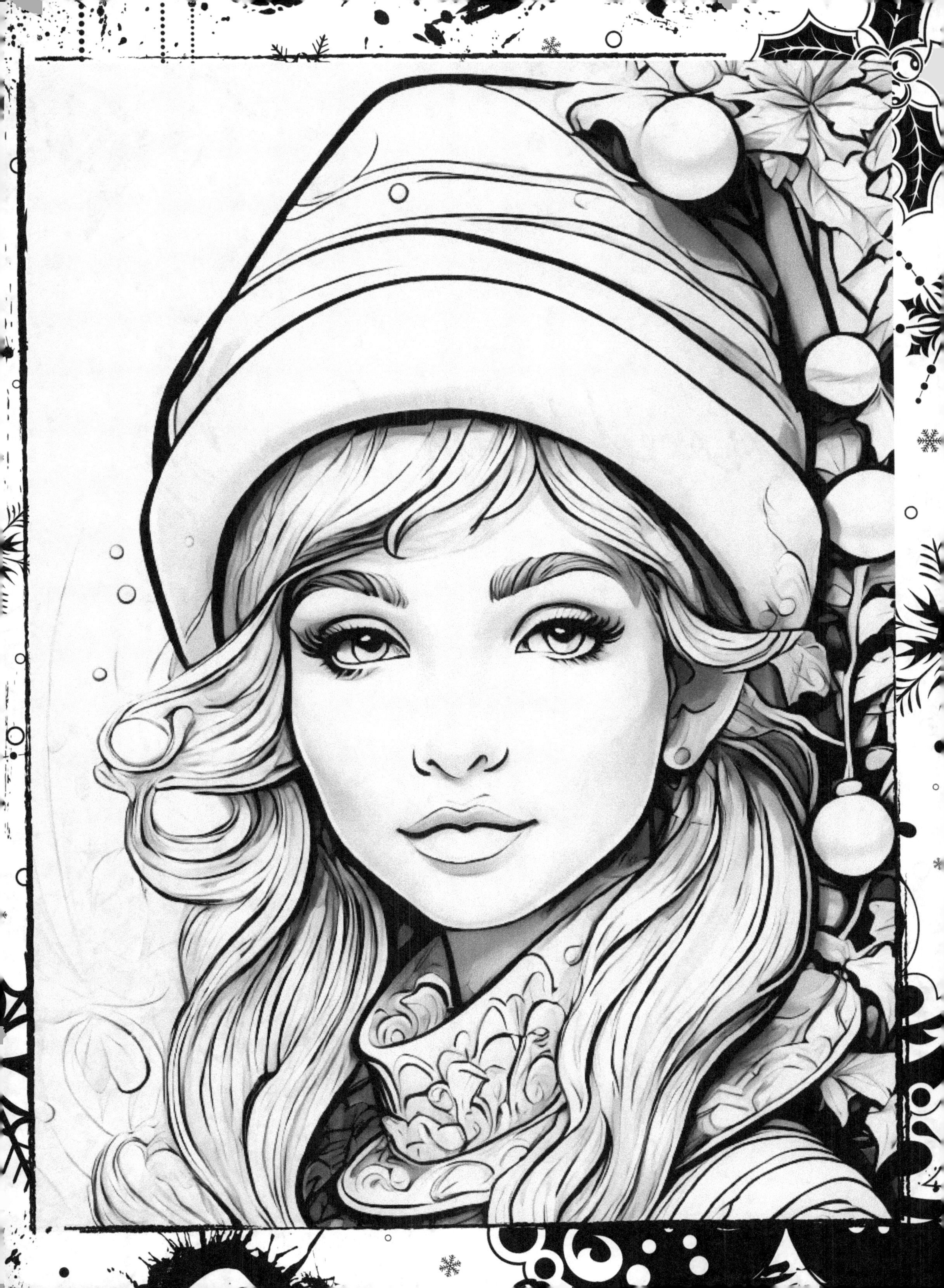

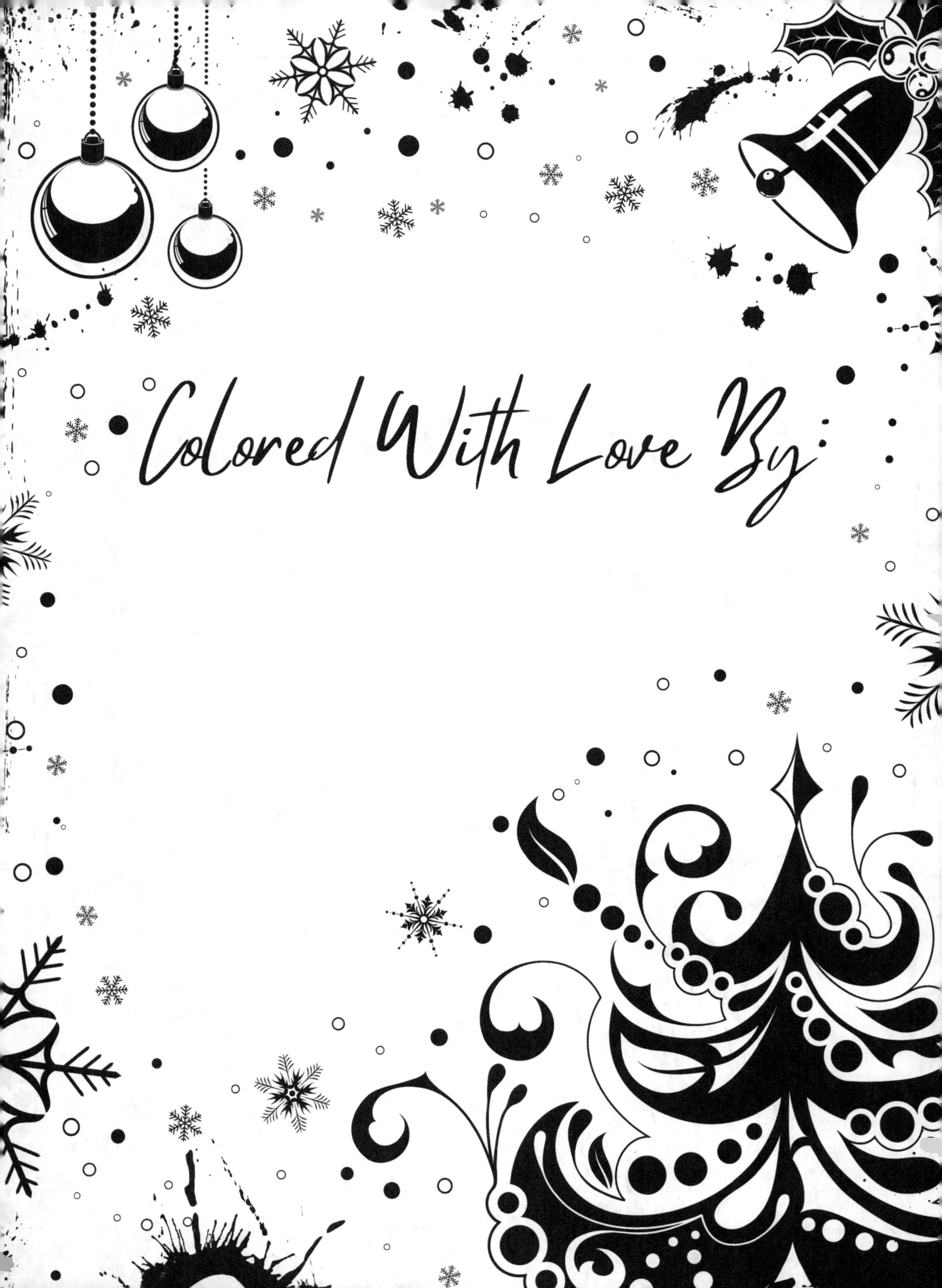
Colored With Love By:

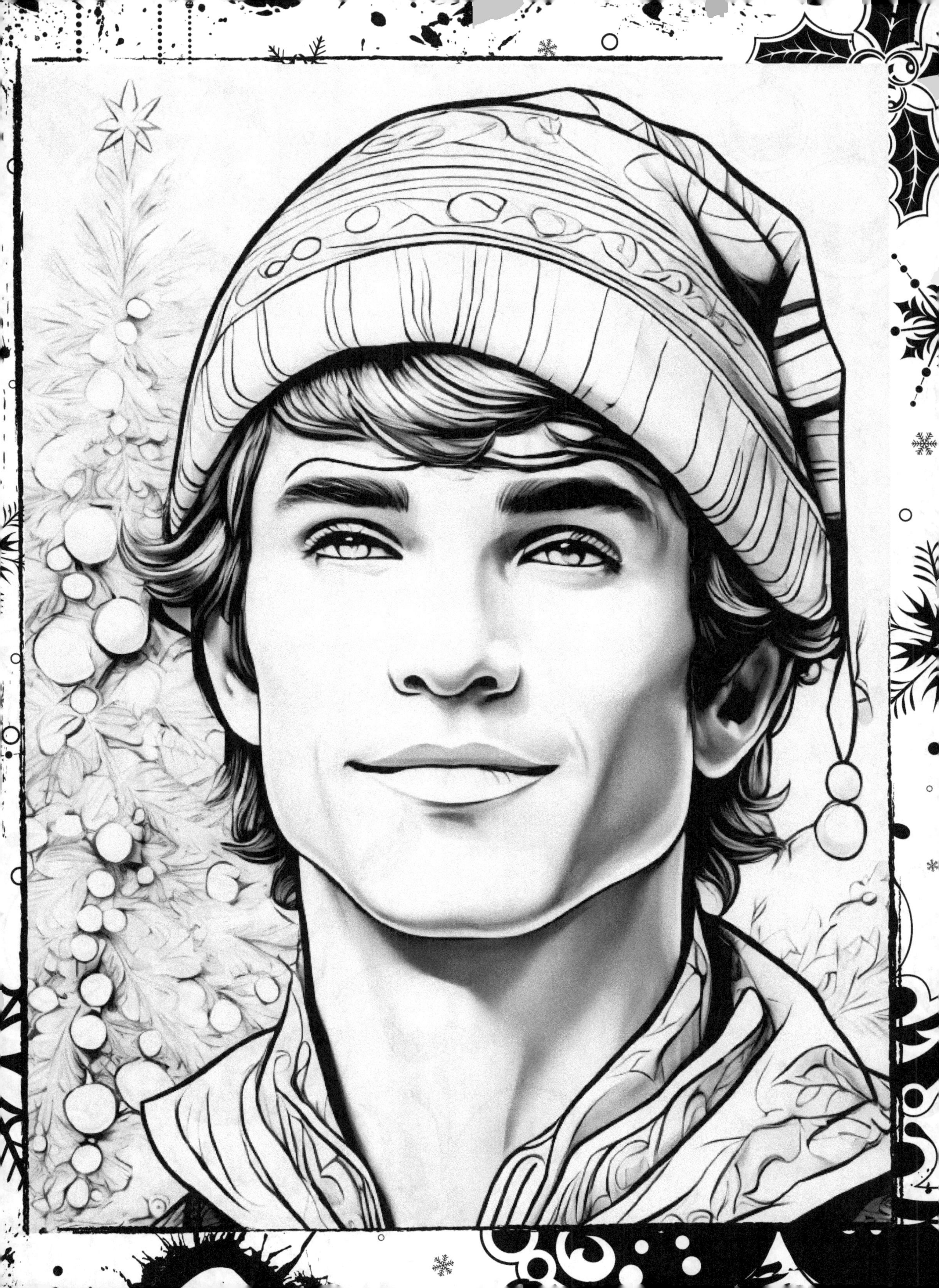

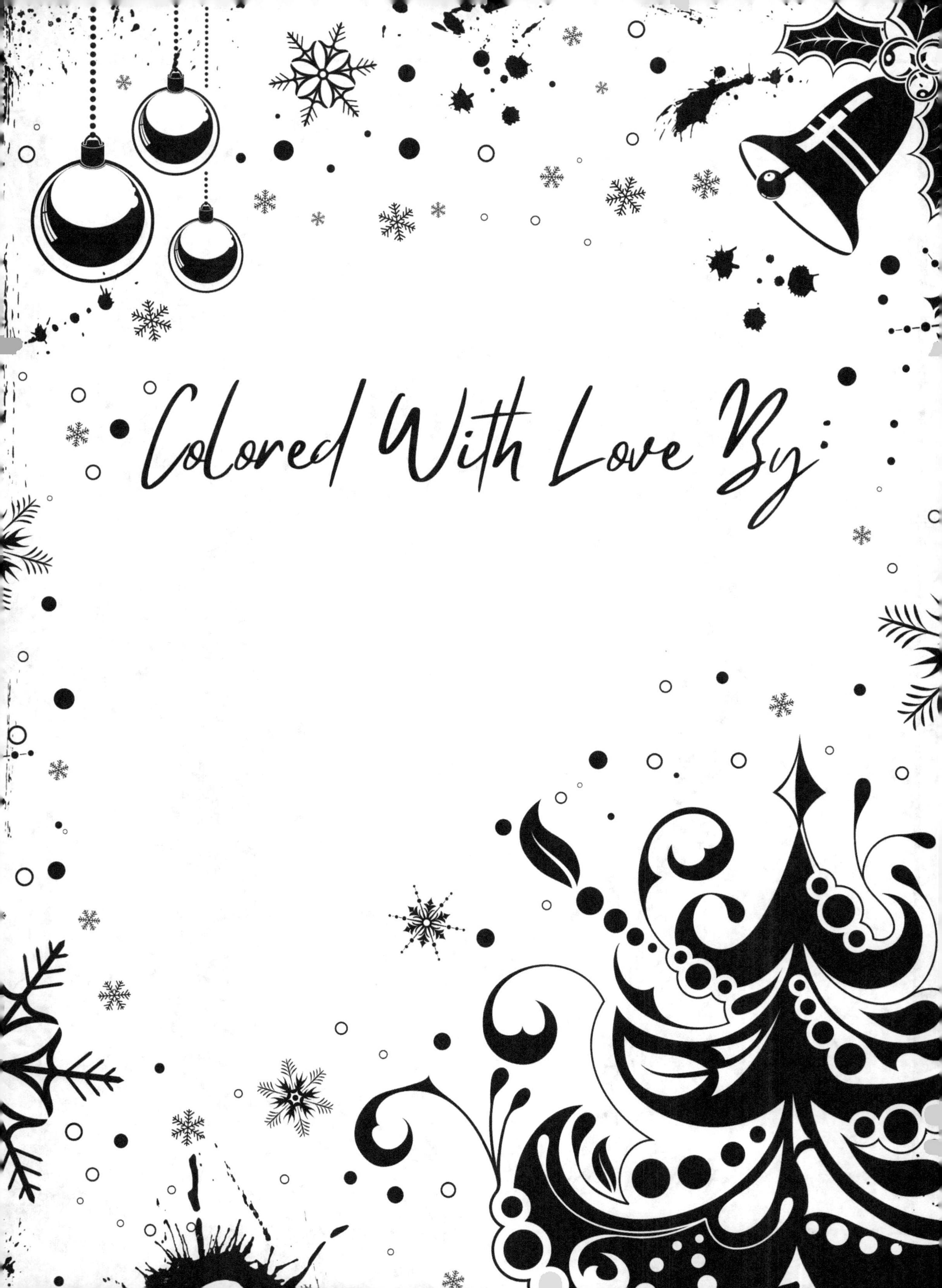

Colored With Love By:

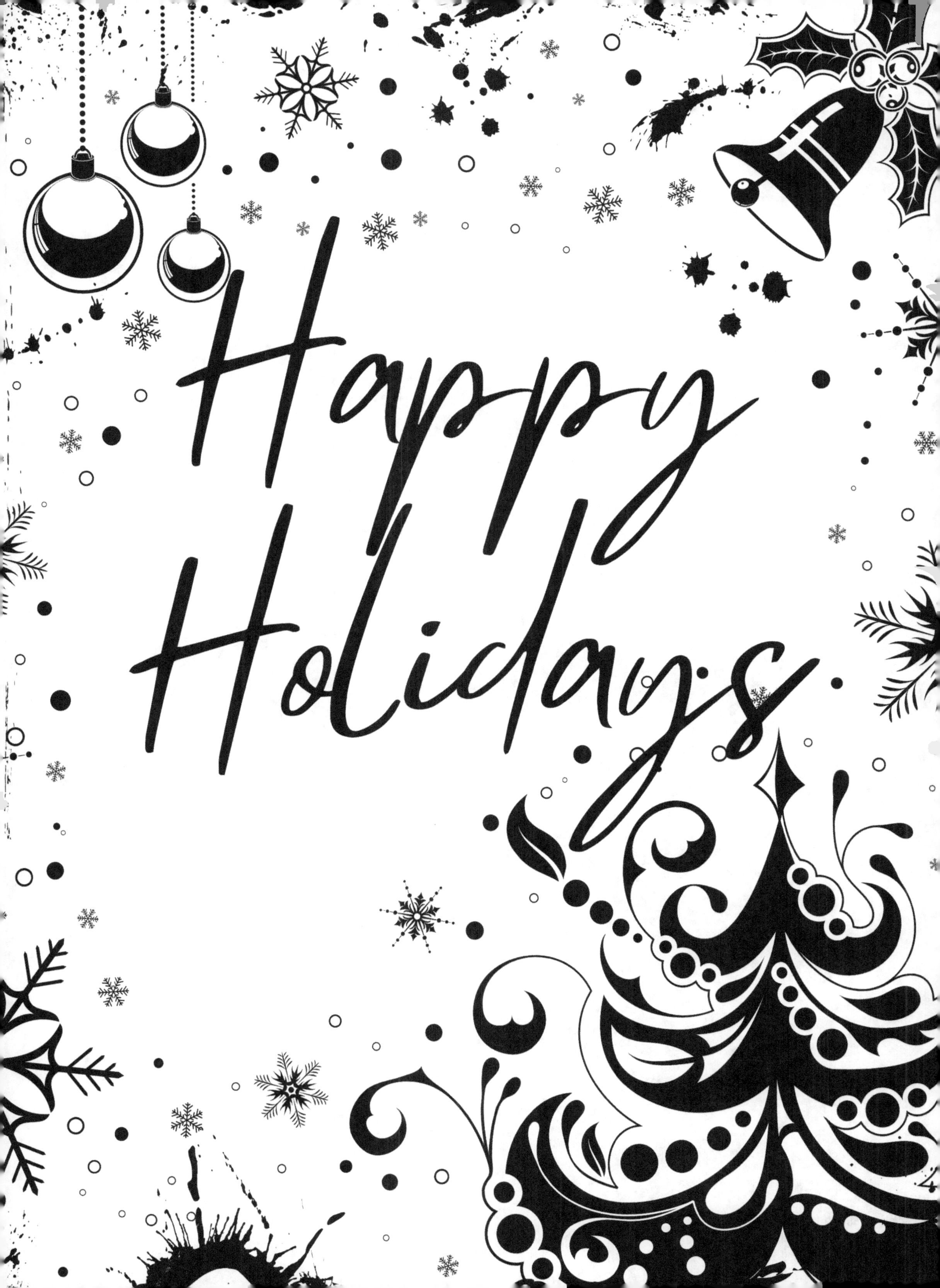
Happy Holidays